A Teen Girl's Guide To Getting Off

A Teen Girl's Guide To Getting Off

By

Eva Sless
© 2016

Published in Australia in 2017 by;
La Bouche Books
www.labouchebooks.com

© 2016, Eva Sless

ISBN 978-0-9923514-2-7 (paperback)
ISBN 978-0-9923514-3-4 (ebook)

Cover art © 2016, Cathy Larsen
Cover Design © 2016, Cathy Larsen, and La Bouche Books

Editor; KL Joy, Rachel Tsoumbakos

Medical Images, Author image © 2016, Joanne O'Keeffe
Character Illustration, © 2016 Cathy Larsen
Girl with Toys images, © 2016, E. Sless
The Great Wall of Vagina – panel 4, © 2011, Jamie McCartney

Produced by;
Ingram Spark

Cataloguing-in-Publication;

Creator: Sless, Eva, author.

Title: A teen girl's guide to getting off / Eva Sless ; edited by
  KL Joy, Rachel Tsoumbakis ; Joanne O'Keeffe ; Cathy Larsen.

ISBN: 9780992351427 (paperback)

Target Audience: For young adults.

Subjects: Teenage girls--Growth. Puberty. Adolescence.

Other Creators/Contributors:
 Joy, K. L., editor.
 Tsoumbakis, Rachel, editor.
 O'Keeffe, Joanne, illustrator, photographer.
 Larsen, Cathy, illustrator.

Dedicated to my Abster.

May your life always be filled with positivity and pleasure.

Acknowledgements;

Thank you to:

My Jman. For always loving me for me and for taking this crazy ride with me.

My parents. For their unconditional love, support, and pride

To every girl who reached out to me in one way or another and said "I need this book". Look look! I made it just for you!

To KL, Grant, Cathy, Jo, and Rachel. This would never have happened without you.

Delaney, Cindy and Eleanor, thank you for making my cis-brained words come out right.

To Martine, who got my head in the right spot and my steps in the right order.

To the People people, to Pauline, to Hayley and to everyone who ever published and printed and believed in my words.

And to chocolate and coffee. You know I could never survive without you.

Preface:

For Parents, or;

Why the Hell am I Writing This Book?

When I was a teenager, and probably when you were too, there were no books out there about sex. Not really anyway. The educational books, like *Where Did I Come From?* and *What's Happening To Me?* were all very well and good, but they were just basic biology. They didn't talk about the things I wanted to know about. Like masturbation and orgasms and pleasure. I remember a friend's mum had *The Joy of Sex* but even that, without the context of knowledge about things like orgasms and sexual pleasure, wasn't much more than a giggle session and a bit of visual stimulation.

The Young Adult books that had sex in them weren't much better either. There was *Forever* by Judy Blume which looked at the budding sexual relationship between a boyfriend and girlfriend (I remember he called his penis Ralph and my friends and I thought that was hilarious) but it was very much about "being with the one person" and "having to be in love first" which I found a bit crap, because I wasn't in love with anyone, but I still wanted to have sex. Then there was *Puberty Blues*, the bestselling book about the culture of Australian teenagers in the late 70s. That book had plenty of sex in it. Plenty! But the message was clear. Only the popular girls can get away with having sex. Anyone else was just a moll and a dirty slut and could be laughed at, mistreated and left in a gutter. Charming.

A little bit later came the *Secret Diary of Laura Palmer*,

a spin off book from the popular 90s series *Twin Peaks*. That was a pretty sexy book. I have since found out I wasn't the only girl of my age who used that book as an accompaniment to masturbation. It was full of underground, dirty anonymous sex, prostitution, drugs, bondage and girl on girl action. It was awesome! But it still had the underlying message that girls who like sex are bad and will probably end up dead, wrapped in plastic, with a strange dancing midget and a supernatural force of evil possessing your family members.

Probably the best, most educational and real sex advice I ever got from when I was a teenager, was from a bunch of comic books called *Streetwize*[1]. These were free comics written between 1984 to 1996 and distributed to schools, youth centres, health centres and the like which dealt with everything from Aboriginal issues, to drugs, sex, acceptance and all the teenage issues that come from being, well, a teenager. It was real and honest and sometimes quite confronting. Yes, there were tales of teenage pregnancy and drug overdoses and STIs, but never the message of *Don't Do It!*. Just the message of, if you're going to, here is how to be safe, minimise harm and risk, and maximise the enjoyment. It was factual, always had a wealth of resources, phone numbers and suggested places you could go to talk about whatever it was you needed to talk about. It was so non-judgemental and accepting it was like having an older friend to talk to and tell you all the shit your mum was too afraid to

I remember a few parents at my high school got a bit offended by them and wanted the school to stop providing them, to which the school politely, but correctly, refused to do.

We are now over a decade into the new millennium and there is still very little out there that not only educates and informs, but normalises all the sex thoughts and curiosity teenage girls have. Because, let's face it, they do have them. They always had them, and all the teenagers and young girls coming up in the world behind them will have them too.

---

1   Streetwize was produced in NSW by the Redfern Legal Centre and can be found here at http://trove.nla.gov.au/work/18725199?selectedversion=NBD3705896

Sure you can search *Dolly Doctor* and learn that discharge is normal, you can read a *Cosmo* and find out *How to get the most from your orgasm* and you can look on the internet for pretty much anything you could ever possibly want to know (and probably a bunch of stuff you wish you'd never heard of) but to have it all in one book, laid out frankly and smartly and in a way that will never judge no matter how "abnormal" you think you are. Well, I've looked, and I've found very, very little on the subject.

In fact, from what I have seen out there, on bookshelves, TV and in magazines and the things people talk about, sex education for girls has gone backwards. We seem to have stagnated in the "good girls don't have sex" school of thought with information and education almost halting at "abstinence" and slut-shaming anyone who dares to think about sex a little more openly.

But the thing is, teenagers are going to have sex. They are. They have been for years. I know. I was one of them and so were most of my friends. I don't know why some people seem to grow up and forget they themselves were experimental, curious and sexual creatures as teenagers. Maybe it's the "fuddy-duddy" gene kicking in. I don't know. I'm just glad I don't have it, and you may not have it either, you may just struggle to find the right way to bring it up. I understand that. It can be a tricky topic to broach. Test the waters with your kids. Don't be afraid to try and open up communication. Even if you're watching a TV show with them and something about sex comes up in it, ask them if they have any questions. Ask them if they talk about sex at school, or if they have had any sex education in their classes. Read this book and then pass it on to them. Let them know you are open to questions. Or, if it's something that makes you uncomfortable to talk about, it's okay to tell them that too. It's okay to tell them that you're not sure of all the answers. It's okay to tell them that you don't know. What isn't okay is pretending their curiosity doesn't exist.

This is the first step to them being closed off and never coming to you. Trust me, the last thing you want as a parent is to be the last to know when something happens that could have been prevented by open communication and education. And these things do happen, and are happening far more frequently and severely. Because of this lack of communication and information for young people, STI rates have risen critically in the past twenty years, teenage pregnancies have become not only rampant but almost celebrated in some kind of morbid "look at the freak show" way in TV shows such as *16 and Pregnant* and *Teen Mom*, and the idea of "sexualising" teenagers and children has made people afraid to even mention the idea of sex for pleasure around young people because they're worried their kids are going to run off and become strippers or porn stars.

Well, I can assure you, telling your kids about sex, pleasure, consent and relationships will not cause this. Okay sure, you never know, your kid may decide they want to be a sex worker later in life, but it's not going to happen just because they decided to have sex when they were a teenager. If that was the case, almost every female in the world would work in the sex industry, and they don't. And the ones who do, do so for a myriad of reasons, very few being because they had sex when they were in high school.

From masturbation and sex toys to doing it and enjoying it and all the safety tips, health tips and enjoyment tips in between. From fantasy and porn to sexting and gossip. Slut-shaming, coming out and experimentation. This book has it all and I, your big sister sexpert, will guide you and your kids through it all. I can't make their pimples go away and I can't stop that hideous first heartbreak they will go through (hey, it's life, we all have at least one heartbreak story) but I will help them understand their body and what it can do. I will explain all that stuff their sex-ed teacher won't, or can't because of school restrictions, and the stuff that you might not know how to. I will do everything I can to help your kids go into the world of sex happy, confident and assured that they are normal, beautiful and ready for what comes at them.

I can do this because I went through it all. The awkwardness. The fumbling. The lack of confidence about my body and the way I looked. The wondering if I was normal. The confusion as to what the hell I was doing. Was I doing it right? Was I doing it wrong? The curiosity and all the wonder about this crazy thing called sex that we were expected to know all about and nothing about at the same time. I went through it all, and I got through it. I got through it and am a happy, settled, confident, independent, strong, powerful woman who knows herself, knows her body, and knows that the journey through puberty can be hell without a friend who knows a bit more than you.

Your kids will get through it too. All they need is some education, some information and someone to lay it all out for them in a way they can relate to and understand. A friend, an older sister, an agony aunt. Someone they can trust who will give them the real deal information they crave. So, that is why I wrote this book. To make their journey a little easier, a lot more informed and heaps more fun.

I would also like to point out that I did not write this book alone. I had plenty of help and feedback from young women I know, and been introduced to by the ones I know. Over the course of two years I spoke to around a hundred young women about their thoughts, feelings and experiences with sex. Their words are dotted around this book and offer a great insight into how we, as women and girls, think about sex and sexuality. It is to all those young women that I emailed and Skyped and Facebooked and met in person that I thank.

Thank you for making this a fun, funny and an eye-opening experience even for me. I hope your future sex lives are fantastic and enjoyable!

This is a book for young, cis-gender women who feel they have not got the best or most informative sex education they deserve. This is not meant to exclude or discriminate against young trans people at all. In fact, it is actually the exact opposite. I am not a trans person. I have never been, nor will I ever be trans. I don't believe, no matter what my experience in the world of sex and my own personal journey, that I have any right whatsoever to speak for young trans women and their bodies at all. In the section of this book where these things are discussed I had a lot of help from my wonderful trans friends ranging in ages from 19 to 50, and I thank them immensely for their time and patience with me.

I truly believe that what is needed now is a series of books just like this one, written by people who know their shit. We need a book for young men, a book for young trans women and a book for young trans men, and we need them now.

SIDE NOTE TO ALL THE BOYS WHO HAVE PICKED THIS BOOK UP...

Good for you! I know, I know. You probably picked this up so you could look at pictures of boobs and vaginas and laugh with your mates. That's cool. That's something we've all done, yes. Even me. But you know what? Here is the chance for you to learn all about sex and girls and how to become an excellent boyfriend and lover. Take your time to actually read this book. Take the time to learn about women's bodies. To learn about consent and respect and what it really means to have sex and "get off". Take a moment to understand that sex is about the both of you. It's about mutual enjoyment and mutual respect. Trust me. You read this book and take it all on board. You'll grow into an exceptional man and a wonderful person to have sex with.

Introduction.

Sex. What a huge topic it is right? There's probably nothing you've ever come across (except maybe talk on drugs) that has the amount of taboo, and misinformation and downright brick-walling surrounding it.

There's nothing else in the world that is so common and normal — and experienced by almost everyone on the planet at some stage — that is met with such resistance and lack of communication.

As an adult, I believe we have a responsibility to teach the younger generations how to navigate the world. We teach you how to dress, how to cook, how to read, how to count. We teach you how to use a toilet, how to look after yourself. We teach you how to use a computer (and then you usually end up teaching us) and we teach you how to drive a car. It would be dangerous and irresponsible of us as parents, guardians, educators and guides to send you out into the world without knowing these things.

And yet when it comes to sex so many parents seem to back off, to clam up and shut down.

So many young people receive only the most basic forms of sex education, usually with the underlying lesson of "don't do it", and then you are sent out into the world and expected to know what you are doing, how to be safe, how to navigate and negotiate relationships and situations and then, when you get it wrong and something happens that is less than desirable you are so often blamed and shamed and dismissed.

It's actually disgusting and so very wrong. It is a failure to you as young adults to not give you all the tools you need to build happy, healthy and successful relationships and, very importantly, enjoyable sexual experiences.

In primary school you probably learnt about the life-cycle of a frog or a tree or something. In high school you may have learnt about puberty and human reproduction and, if you were lucky, you may have got a banana to put a condom on.

But sex is so much more than frog spawn and condoms on bananas. It is a massive world of confusion, questions, trial and error.

The way we teach sex to young people right now is so fraught with danger it would be like me giving you the keys to a Lamborghini and telling you to go for it, without teaching you how to drive first.

Because that's the thing, sex is a little bit like driving a car.

You cannot get those keys, jump in your car and expect to be the Stig on your first go. That would end up in you and your shiny car being wrapped around a tree and you probably dead. Before we even let you inside a car we teach you the basics of safety and the rules of the road. You need to know where the key goes, where your mirrors are. You need to get a feel for the seats, for the steering wheel. You need to know how to indicate, how to change gears, how to watch for other drivers. Then you need to start slowly. You drive around a car park for a while getting used to bunny hops and stalling. How heavy the car is, how hard you turn the wheel and push on the brakes.

After a few jittery car park goes you can start going around the slow back streets and learning how round-a-bouts work, and how to watch the traffic and world around you. You have a guide and a teacher with you showing you how to navigate the roads and the powerful machine you are now in charge of.

It can be scary. You will make mistakes, but with proper guidance you'll soon get the hang of it and then you are ready for a night drive, a rainy drive, a foggy drive. You start to bring other passengers into your car but you're still under the careful guide of your teacher making sure that you're safe, that your passengers are safe. It's a long process, but one that is absolutely necessary so that when you finally get your P plates and go off alone for the very first time, you are mostly confident that you and your friends will be safe, and you'll bring the car home without a ding on it.

Now let's look at that analogy as sex. Your body is the big important machine, and you need to know exactly how to look after it and use it and how it works so that you can confidently drive it and enjoy it and, one day, allow passengers in it and make sure that everyone has a safe and enjoyable journey.

All the things that make your body work, that make sex an enjoyable and satisfying experience come with practice and with knowledge. Just knowing how a frog lays eggs and that girls bleed out of their vaginas every month is not enough to teach you or prepare you for the huge number of factors that come into play with sex, sexuality and sexual experiences.

That's like me giving you a car key and a road map and letting you take your little brother to school because I know you've watched *The Fast and The Furious*. It's utterly ridiculous and it is dangerous as hell.

I wrote this book because I have seen first hand the damage the current school system is doing with their lack of proper sex education. In my line of work I speak to young women daily who have been given the keys to their machine and have crashed it somehow. They have gotten pregnant, sick, confused, hurt, and ashamed. They have no idea that their journeys are supposed to be fun, that learning how to drive it properly could be some of the most satisfying and pleasurable experiences they'll ever have.

They've been told that they're bad, wrong, slutty, dirty. That if something went wrong, it's most likely their own fault.

I want to change this.

I want young women like you to learn exactly what their car is capable of. I want to teach you how to drive it, how to navigate the roads it will take. I want to make sure that when you finally allow a passenger into your car you are prepared and confident and able to make the right choices. I want you to know what every button, switch and knob in your car is for so that you can get the best experiences out of it, because there is no way you will ever have a satisfying drive with someone else if you don't know how to drive solo and look after your own car.

Anyway, enough with the car analogies, let's get on with it.

Ch-Ch-Ch-Ch-Changes
Ah Puberty...

As the great man, David Bowie, once said:

"Turn and face the strange."

Look, I'm not going to go on and on about how your body is entering womanhood and how wonderful and amazing it is. I'm not going to spoon feed you a bunch of lines about the beauty of growing up because, quite frankly, I think that's a load of shit. It's exciting, yes. It's different, yes. It will change you, yes. But while you're going through it it's a bit shit a lot of the time. Growth spurts and the inevitable clumsiness that comes with it; banging into things, tripping over your ever growing legs and feet. Confusing mood swings where one minute you are giddy with excitement over a boy, then the next minute you want to sob like you've never sobbed before because your best friend hasn't answered your latest text. The next you can't slam the door hard enough to show your mum just how fricken pissed off you are because she won't let you go to the party all your mates are going to ... and all within about half an hour of each other.

And don't let me go on too much about getting your period. That can be totally sucky.

See, when you're a teenager all sorts of crazy things start to happen and change. Your body shape, the way your body works, your brain, the way you look at things and view the world. It can be a bit of a roller coaster ride; fun, scary, up and down and a whole lot of "what the fuck is going on!?"

You know what the worst thing is? When someone dismisses you by saying something like, "Oh, it's just puberty. You'll be right," because, the thing is, when you're going through it, you don't really know. I mean, sure you know you're changing and you know what the word for it is, but it's so gradual it sort of creeps up on you. Like growing your hair, you don't see it growing. You don't really think you look any different to the day you got it cut, until you see a photo six months later and think, "Wow, my hair really HAS grown!"

It's the same with puberty. It doesn't matter if everyone else can tell, to you its just life. Just normal. Just another day. It's not like you wake up one morning and say, "Oh, golly gee! Today I have hit, 'The Puberty', I feel different all over! I must be becoming a woman." No. It doesn't work that way and anyone giving you that, "It's just puberty" brush off has obviously forgotten what it was like.

It's not just physical changes either. The whole world begins to look different. Your parents turn into horrible creatures full of rules and ways to embarrass you. Friendship groups begin to change and so can your interests, beliefs and ideas.

The hardest thing about it all; the body changes, the mood swings, the zits, growth spurts, periods, boobs, all of it, is it's basically out of your control. There's nothing you can do to stop it and that can really suck. The main thing to remember (even though while you're going through it it's a bit of useless advice that means very little) is it doesn't last forever. It does settle down. Another piece of useless advice I will give you is you're not alone. Everyone else you know is going through it too; in different ways, with different results and different ways of dealing with it. Even the coolest, most with-it chick in your class is going through it. It's inevitable. It's puberty. It's life. Knowing this won't make it any better. It still sucks and feels like you're the only one in the world who knows what it's really like, but I figure I'll tell you anyway because that's my job.

You see, while one girl is stressing out that she'll never grow boobs another is hating the fact that hers are bigger than everyone elses in the class. While one girl looks at her pimply face in the morning and thinks the world is ending, another is freaking out because she still hasn't got her period. Like I keep saying throughout this book, everyone is different and goes through it all in different ways, but regardless of if your boobs don't grow til you're 17 or you got your first period when you were 11, it's all normal. All of it. If you really think something is wrong then it is really important to go and talk to a doctor. There is a section in the Body Care bit of this book all about seeing doctors.

Here are some of the most common things that happen during puberty. They can happen at different stages and at different ages and at different rates, so again, don't stress out too much if it happens earlier or later than your mates. It's just the way we are. Different.

Body Shape

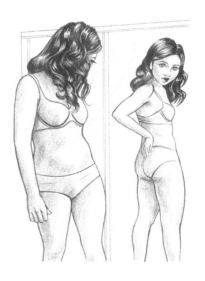

From about the age of 11-12 (but, like I said, sometimes it's earlier, sometimes it's later) your body begins to change shape. Your hips widen, your boobs grow, and the shape of your face changes and you can get really achy arms and legs from fast growth spurts. Growth spurts usually happen earlier for girls than guys which is why you often see from around year five to year eight a bunch of tall, leggy girls towering over the boys, but the guys usually catch up by about year nine.

Boobs

On the subject of boobs, they start to grow from about the age of eleven. It can be a slow, gradual thing, or they can spring out quite fast. Buying your first bra can be a fun experience, but it can also be a rather embarrassing one. I remember when my mum took me to get my first bra. I was pretty young, about eleven, and was one of the first girls in my grade to need one. The lady at the shop was rather grabby (not in a sexual way or anything, just not very sensitive to the fact it was a completely humiliating experience for me) and made comments like, "Golly, you ARE a big girl for your age aren't you?" Totally mortifying! Really not what I needed to hear as a girl who was already self conscious about the changes I was going through faster than most of my friends. My mum, bless her, seemed to sense my discomfort and kind of bustled her out of the change room telling her we would be fine on our own, but I never forgot that experience. A really good friend told me a similar story about her first bra except the lady kind of peered at her rather flat-ish chest and told her she probably didn't even need one as she was so small. She was sixteen and desperate to wear one like all her mates. Yes, she was small, but it didn't mean she didn't need one. Sometimes these things can be psychological as well as physical. Fitting in is one of the most important desires when you're a teenager.

These days (from what I am told) bra sales assistants are much more politically correct and sensitive and don't make a habit of shaming girls who are bigger or smaller than the rest, but I do suggest going with someone you trust like an older sister, your mum, or a friend.

Another thing about growing boobs is that a lot of the time they grow at different rates. Sometimes it is barely noticeable and other times it's pretty obvious that one of your boobs is an A cup and the other a C. This usually sorts itself out, but if it doesn't, or if it's really, really noticeable, there are certain steps you can take. Those chicken fillet inserts can be good, padded bras too. However, like in all cases, if you are worried about anything your body is doing and think there is a problem, please talk to a doctor you trust.

Hair.

Pubic hair. Armpit hair. Leg hair. Facial hair. When you go through puberty you get kinda hairy. The fine hairs on your legs start to thicken. Coarse, curly hair grows around the lips of your vagina and on your pubic bone and sometimes crawls up towards your belly button. Hair sprouts from your armpits and you can even get a darkening of hair on your upper lip, chin and sideburns. It's okay. You're not turning into a guy. It's just hormones. It's perfectly normal. BUT it doesn't make it less annoying or embarrassing for some girls. If it really does bother you, there are quite a few things you can do to help reduce body hair. There are creams and waxing and even laser treatments. Talk to someone in a chemist or beauty salon to see if they are able to help you out and make it a bit easier to deal with.

Discharge

Have you started to notice strange gloopy stuff in your undies? Sometimes it's quite clear with the consistency of egg white, and other times it might be a bit thicker, kind of like Clag glue. Sometimes there's a lot, and other times not so much, but the older you get the more you're going to start noticing it.

Don't panic. This is (for the most part) completely normal. As you'll read in the section about vaginas, the vagina is a pretty fantastic body bit that can do all sorts of things, including keeping itself clean, and this is basically what this discharge is. It's a perfectly normal and natural process of keeping the vagina clean and maintaining the natural balance of things. Depending on your menstrual cycle, the consistency changes. Just after ovulation, when you're super fertile and your body is getting ready to get pregnant, it is the clear, stringy sort. This helps sperm reach the eggs. And in your less fertile moments it is the thicker consistency.

Pretty much the only real problem with discharge is that it can stain and sometimes discolour your undies. If you find it an issue the best way to save your pants is to use panty liners. These are like pads you wear for a period but a lot thinner and are designed to keep your knickers fresh and clean from discharge. Whatever you do, do not douche to get rid of it. This causes all sorts of problems which are talked about later in the vagina section.

Normal discharge doesn't really have too much of a smell, beyond the normal smells of a vagina, so if you notice that the discharge has a strong odour (often quite fishy) or changes colour and becomes yellowish, or grey, or looks a bit like lumpy cottage cheese, it's very likely you could have an infection or vaginal problem. Check out the section on STIs for more information on the changes within your body of certain sexually transmitted infections and imbalances that can occur.

Periods.

Probably one of the biggest, most important and (if I do say so myself) most irritating parts of being a female and going through puberty is getting your period. I don't care what all those other books and things say about "becoming a woman" and whatever other flowery bullshit they feed you. Getting your period can be totally shit. It's painful with cramps. It screws up your already bouncing moods. It can be embarrassingly obvious if you accidentally leak through your clothes and, well, to put it bluntly, there's nothing "beautiful" or "magical" about bleeding out of your vagina for a week.

Yes, it is exciting. Yes, it's a huge step in your growth. Yes, it is probably the one thing most girls look at as the biggest change you will have ever gone through in your life up to this point. But it's still bloody (pardon the pun) irritating.

LGBTIQA stuff

While many of us already kind of know from a pretty early age which side of the sexuality fence we sit on, for others it's not so clear, and puberty is a time when, even if we *think* we know, our bodies and the hormones flowing through them like to confuse us even more. Questioning your sexuality and preferences is completely normal at this time in your life. It's confusing and can lead to all sorts of inner questions. When I was about 12 or 13 I remember having one of the sexiest, most delicious dreams ever. Up until then I thought only boys could have "wet dreams" but I had one, and it was amazing. But the main player in my dream, the object of my desire, was a girl from a TV show I watched. A girl! I'd never even really thought about girls up until then, it was all about boys and penises. As I grew older and had more experiences I found I really was rather attracted to girls, although my main focus was, and still is, on guys. Discovering new sides to yourself is what this crazy journey called life is all about. The best advice I can give you about this is to go with the flow and let yourself experience and feel what you feel. Everything we do in life is trial and error

Everything you think and feel, even the confusing bits you don't quite understand, or can't quite put your finger on, is all normal. Completely. This is the time where the puzzle pieces start to slot together. Sometimes the puzzle is a bit easier to work out than others, but it's always a work in progress.

Before we go on, I also want to point out the huge difference between "sexuality" and "gender". They are often lumped in together as one and the same, but they aren't. In the most basic of terms "sexuality" is about attraction and desire. It's about who you want to be with, kiss, sleep with, be intimate with, and form a relationship with. "Gender," on the other hand, is about how we relate to ourselves and how we identify ourselves as male, female, or somewhere on the sliding scales between.

LGBTIQA stands for; Lesbian, Gay, Bisexual, Transgender, Intersex, Queer, Asexual.

Let's break it down letter by letter;

Lesbian – Girls who are sexually attracted to girls

Gay – Boys who are sexually attracted to boys

Bisexual – Girls and boys who are sexually attracted to both girls and boys

Transgender (once known as Transsexual) – Transsexual is an outdated term and can be really offensive. This is mostly because being Trans has absolutely nothing to do with sexuality. The correct term is Transgender because it is how the individual identifies with themselves and their gender versus the genitals they have and the gender they were assigned at birth. Regardless of what (if any) gender you are sexually attracted to.

Intersex — someone whose sex characteristics are neither exclusively male nor female. This can be in their genitals, in their hormones and chromosomes, and in their secondary sex characteristics such as the way we develop and change during puberty. Intersex does not necessarily mean that the person has two different genitals, or deformed genitals, it is far more likely to be hormonal and to do with the brain and the chemicals our hormones produce.

Queer – The umbrella term that covers all non-heterosexual and/or non-cisgendered people (cissexual is the term used for people who are born as the same gender they identify with)

Asexual – People who are not sexually attracted or oriented to anyone of any gender.

Another letter in this rainbow of sexuality and gender stuff that isn't mentioned in the above acronym is P for **Pansexual**.

Pansexuality is when you are sexually attracted to people of all the letters of the rainbow. It is neither a male nor female thing nor a gay or lesbian thing. For a pansexual, gender and sexuality are irrelevant to sexual attraction.

Gender Fluidity

People who identify as being gender fluid do not necessarily identify with one gender or the other, regardless of what genitals they may have. In fact gender fluidity has nothing at all to do with genitals at all, that's kind of the point.

"I knew I was a lesbian before I knew what a lesbian was. I remember when I was about four I wanted to marry my kindy teacher and have a baby with her" — Deb, 17

"I have this big crush on a girl at school. I don't know if I'm gay. I just know I want to kiss her. I've kissed boys before too." — Helen, 15

"I've been confused about it since I was about 13. I'm still torn between asexual and bisexual. I think I decided to stick with Bi-Romantic Asexual when I was about 15" — Heather, 16

Because there are so many terms and people identify as so many different things I will just use the blanket term Queer to keep it all a bit simpler and easier to understand.

Like I mentioned before, puberty and growing up and all that stuff is hard. Really hard. And when you add into the mix all the stresses and confusions that come with sex and sexuality with being queer it can be an even more tricky time. I mean, just trying to figure out all the things about sex when you're a teenager is hard enough and then when you add into the mix that a lot of straight teenagers (and adults) have queer sex dreams and fantasies and crushes, trying to put labels and identities onto all that can make growing up even more confusing. In a perfect world sexuality and who you are attracted to or how you feel about your body and sexuality shouldn't even be an issue. Unfortunately, however, this is not a perfect world and there are some people about who have a really hard time understanding and accepting not everyone is heterosexual. This puts horrible pressure on you when you are a queer teenager who just wants to get on with the actual stuff of growing up like pimples and crushes and homework assignments.

Some people know from the earliest age they can remember that they are queer. Some don't really know at all because they haven't put words or labels to it or just haven't felt they needed to put a box or frame around themselves. There is no right or wrong way to work out how you feel about your sexuality, it is different for every person who goes through it. The one thing to remember though, regardless of whether you are queer or straight or not really all that sure yet is you are normal. Perfectly 100% normal. You are not sick. You are not a freak. You are not rebelling. You may be a little confused about how to figure it all out but like I said, everyone is confused during puberty so it's all just part of the way you are and how everyone is. It sucks you will have to defend yourself for being you and answer stupid questions from people who think it's any of their business who you decide to fall in love with or have a crush on or any of that. I mean, no one asks hetero people, "when did you first know you were straight?" Or, "why did you choose to be straight?" So to a lot of people (and ever growing more people) the whole idea of having to identify yourself to please someone else's insecurities or confusion is a bit ridiculous. But, like I said before, this is not a perfect world, and there are always going to be people who believe it is their moral duty or right to question and judge and treat you like a piece of shit just because you happen to not fall into their little box of "people are this way and that's the end."

Coming Out

Coming out (telling people you are queer) is hard. It is hard no matter what age you are, but being a teenager and not being sure of what sort of support you will get can be scary and rather isolating. It's always going to be a nerve-wracking decision, but there are a few things that might help make it a little easier for you, if you decide you are ready to tell people. Because, if you don't want to, you don't have to, it is entirely up to you who you tell, when you tell and why you tell.

— Don't feel pressured to come out. It is entirely up to you.

— Find someone you trust. It may not necessarily be your parents or your best friend.

— Be prepared for different reactions. Everything from acceptance to surprise to disbelief to anger

— Try to find a support group to help give advice and support if you need it

— Be aware that once you tell someone, the news may spread pretty fast.

— Don't come out in anger. As in, don't yell it at your parents in the middle of a fight. Don't use it to try and hurt, or win over, or change someone's attitude.

— If someone rejects you once you have told them, try not to let it ruin your own feelings about yourself. Remember, you are normal. You are okay.

— Make sure you feel safe when you come out. If it ends in feeling unsafe (you're threatened or thrown out of home, for example) make sure you have a safe place to go.

Something else I think is really important is to think about what you would do if a friend was to come out to YOU. How you would react, how you would treat them, all that sort of stuff is just as crucial. Just remember, if someone has trusted you enough to put their confidence in you, it is up to you not to break that trust. Not to run about and tell everyone. Think of how it would feel to you, to have finally worked up the courage to tell someone such a large and personal thing, and they treat you like shit and betray your trust.

Friendship is a two-way street and being a good friend is just as valuable as having one.

— *"When I finally came out to my mum she told me she had always kind of known and gave me a hug. It was simple for me. But I know friends who have had a really bad time"* — Deb, 17

— *"My mum was really angry. She cried and told me I was just faking it for attention. That was hard. We are close now, but it did take a while"* — Peta, 17

— *"I walked into the lounge room and straight up told my mum. She completely accepts me. I texted my dad the next day and then slowly came out to the rest of my family with my mum and dad's help. I didn't want to make a big deal of it"* — Heather, 16

— *"I still haven't told anyone. I talk to people on online forums and I have support there. I just don't really know what to say yet."* — Jaz, 15

There are heaps of awesome websites and groups you can access for more help and information. It really is a good idea to look them up and find some support from not only peers (people your own age) but adults who can help you with all your questions and support needs.

Some great websites are:

www.minus18.org.au – Australia wide support, mentoring and mental health services. Social groups. Resources. Networking.

www.pflagaustralia.org.au – Parents and Friends of Lesbian and Gay Australians. A non profit voluntary organisation with the the common goal of keeping families together.

www.lgbthealth.org.au – An Australia wide coalition of health services and health-related organisations targeted at LGBTIQA Australians.

www.samesame.com.au – Support. News. Forums.

www.comingout.com.au – Help and support and information on coming out.

www.asexuality.org – Support, information and advice on asexuality.

http://www.gendercentre.org.au/ — Services for the transgender and gender diverse community.

Getting To Know Your Vagina

So, now we've looked at the changing body work, let's check under the hood (so to speak) of our amazing machines, and see how the engine and all its bits work.

Vagina. Vulva. Fanny. Front Bum. Cunt. Pussy. Yoni. Slit. Punani. Gash. Flower. Hole. Cooter. Coochie. Cherry. Sheath. Honey Pot. Axe Wound. Apple Pie. Muff.

There are so many words to describe your bits! I know while reading that list you will have thought of plenty of others you've heard or use yourself. In fact, it is probably the only thing in the entire universe that has that many names and slang words to describe it. It is both loved and feared by men and women alike and has been blamed for many things including wars and the fall of kings and even, in some cases, natural disasters and strange phenomenon.

Pretty powerful huh? And you have one! That's a bit cool.

Even without all the scary mumbo-jumbo vaginas have apparently caused, the actual real things it can do are pretty fantastic. It brings life into this world. It gives spine tingling pleasure. It helps you to attract a partner (no, not by flashing it around, I will get to this soon). It even cleans itself. It is, simply put, probably the most amazing part of your body aside from your brain.

The following diagram shows your vag in all its glory. Every fold, every flap, every little part of it has its own name and it is a good idea to know them all, where they are and what their purpose is.

The vagina itself is only one part — the tunnel bit where the baby comes out and the tampon goes in and also where your G-Spot is located. The bit you see mostly (the outside lips) is called the vulva and then there are the labias majora and minora (the inner flap bits) the urethra

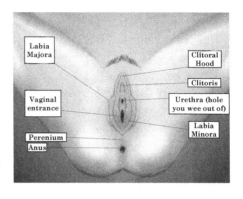

(where wee comes out) and the clitoris (the little button up the top) with its hood (the cover over your clitoris).

The clitoris is one of the best body parts ever. It is the only bit on any human that has no purpose other than to bring pleasure to the owner. It has over 8000 nerve endings and extends from the tip you see, all the way to the base of your spine, and even spreads out through the vulva. It truly is awesome, and getting to know it should be a priority. Without sounding too wanky, your vagina and all the bits and bobs that make it up, should become your BFF. You should love it, nurture it, take care of it and be proud of it. You should learn what it likes, what it doesn't like and what it takes to make it tick. All vaginas are different and respond in different ways so, in all seriousness, if you don't know how to get the best out of it, then it's going to be hard for anyone else to figure it out.

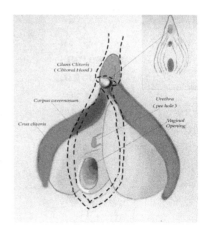

The G-spot

Although it's not something you can see when you look, the G-spot is one very cool part of your vagina that is, like the clitoris, all about pleasure. It can be a little bit tricky to find, and can feel a bit odd at first, but it can seriously lead to some amazingly intense sensations and orgasms. It is located about halfway up the inside of your vagina on the front wall. Kind of like just below where your belly button is. It has a slightly different texture than the rest of your vagina and usually, the harder you push on it, the better it feels. There is more information further on about how to find and play with it and get the best sensations out of it.

I want you to have a look at this amazing plaster cast panel. This is the Great Wall of Vagina, made by British artist Jamie McCartney. It is one section of an incredible piece of art that has the moulds of 400 different vulvas, from women of all ages, sizes and nationalities, including transgender, pre and post natal, and even pre and post labiaplasty (the often unnecessary surgical cutting of labia to make them smaller). It shows that we are all different, and yet all completely normal. Your vulva, your vagina, your bits are included in that. You. Are. Normal.

As you can see in the amazing casts on the vagina wall, every single one is different Some have longer lips, some are wider, and some vary in colour. Each one of these vaginas is normal although, if you have ever looked through an adult magazine, I bet you're thinking yours is wrong, not neat and tucked up like those girls in porn. Let me tell you a little secret. Just like

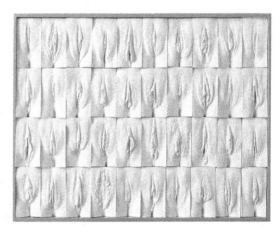

Panel number 4 of 10 of The Great Wall of Vagina
by Jamie McCartney

nearly every other image you see in a magazine, those vaginas are not real. They have been airbrushed and photo-shopped to make sure not a single little bit is poking out. Why? Well here is the kick in the face. In Australia, certain laws and regulations mean it is compulsory for the publication to "smooth" out vaginas and make them look as neat as possible, in fact the publishing industry words it as "healed to a single crease." Why, you ask again? Well, it's simple and rather disturbing. According to the people who are in charge of the things we all get to look at, vaginas in all their folded, lotus-flower-like glory are "indecent". Take a minute for that to sink in. Some bigwig men, with way too much time on their hands and way too much self importance believe your vagina is rude and pornographic.

This, my friends, is bullshit. From the minute you enter puberty your vagina begins to open and change and grow. Things that were once tucked in become more prominent and everything begins to look different. It is *not* indecent. It is *not* rude. It is just your vagina like everyone else in the world who has one. And again, look at the pictures, they are *all* different.

Looking after it.

One of the coolest things about your vagina is the fact that it has the ability to pretty much clean and look after itself. I say pretty much because there are certain things you have to do to help maintain its cleanliness but overall, the inside bits take care of themselves.

Wiping

When you go to the loo, regardless of if you're weeing or pooing, make sure you always wipe front to back. This is to stop bacteria and all the yucky bits from your bum getting inside and stuffing up the natural balance of things.

Washing

When you're in the shower or bath make sure to wipe yourself like you do when in the toilet but whatever you do DO NOT clean the inside of your vagina at all. Seriously. This is bad.

Not only can you hurt yourself, it will wash away vital bacteria and fluids that are there specifically to clean and balance the ph levels inside. This goes for any kind of douching (pushing liquid up inside the vagina). It is absolutely unnecessary and can cause all sorts of issues like thrush and urinary tract infections. Some soaps and body washes can be high in pH levels and can clean away some of the natural bacteria that help keep your vagina healthy so it can be a good idea to use pH balanced washes. You don't have to spend heaps of money on specific "feminine washes" either. Just normal baby bath lotion is a great way to get a good, healthy clean wash.

Grooming

Waxing, shaving, trimming. These are all pretty common practices among women but, apart from some people thinking it makes their vaginas "nicer to look at" it really serves no purpose. In fact, pubic hair itself is quite useful. Firstly it shows that a woman has gone through puberty, therefore being old enough to have sex, bear children and all the other adulty

Cunt.

What a word. It has such power behind it, such force, and is deemed to be probably the most disgusting swear word out there. But in fact the word (like the vagina itself) is not rude, nor disgusting, nor one any girl should shy away from.

The origins of the word cunt are often disputed, but the most common thought is that it comes from the word quna or gwen meaning "queen" and, considering many ancient cultures worshipped female genitalia as life giving and beautiful, this seems pretty fitting.

The very first form of written language is called "cuneiform" and comes from the ancient Sumerian word "kunta" which means female genitalia. Back then (3100BC) women were the keepers of records and written transcripts and the writing itself looks like wedges and mounds that look very much like vulvas.

things our vaginas do. It also helps protect all the sensitive and delicate parts from dust and other outside particles. While keeping those things out, another great thing pubic hair does is help trap pheromones in. These are the unique smells our body gives out and which have been scientifically proven to be what attracts us to compatible mates. I have a bit of a theory as to why certain celebrities have such short marriages. I reckon it's because they wax every inch of hair from themselves so their pheromones are lost in the ether and they are attracting incompatible matches. This is, of course, complete speculation, but it works for me.

On the subject of smells, your vagina has many different scents. These change depending on your menstrual cycle, your sexual arousal and even on what you eat. Some smells are stronger than others but they are usually absolutely normal. I say usually because some strong smells can signal an infection or bacterial imbalance like thrush, so if you're worried have a chat to your doctor. But no matter what you read, or what you are told, there is one truth.

YOUR VAGINA IS MEANT TO SMELL LIKE A VAGINA. Anyone who tries to tell you that it needs to be scented and spritzed and smelling like anything other than a vagina is lying to you.

If a boy has an issue with the smell of vagina then that boy is not ready for grown up sex and should not be anywhere near anyone's vagina.

THE PENIS

We've spent all this time looking at, and taking about, vaginas but if you're a sexually curious heterosexual girl, I'm gonna assume you're pretty curious about penises too. What they look like, feel like, what they do, how they work... All that stuff. So here is your penis 101 class!

The difference between a circumcised and uncircumcised penis is the foreskin. The best way to describe the difference is that a circumcised penis looks like it's wearing a little helmet, and the uncircumcised one looks like it has a long-necked sweater pulled over its head. The differences the foreskin brings are not just limited to

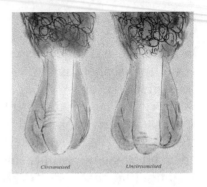
Circumcised   Uncircumcised

look either. Remember how I told you about the clitoris and the thousands and thousands of nerve endings it contains that make it feel really good when touched? Well the penis and foreskin also have these nerve endings. While a clitoris has about 8000 nerve endings, all concentrated in that small nub, the head of the penis has about 4000. The foreskin also has nerve endings and this, matched with the fact that the foreskin covers the sensitive head of the penis, means that uncircumcised penises can be more sensitive to the touch. This is kind of subjective though because most men who are circumcised have it happen when they are very young babies and therefore have no real way of comparing it. Men who have had it done later in life definitely claim to have more sensitivity, but then, that would be in comparison to what they could feel before the operation and, again, makes it very subjective.

The foreskin is also like a little sleeve over the whole penis, so the skin moves independently and can stroke the shaft like an outer casing. This means there are slightly different techniques to playing with and touching one, but it is also, again, subjective to each individual penis. What feels good on one may not on another.

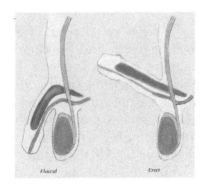
Flaccid   Erect

When sexually aroused the penis fills with blood which causes it to get bigger, and harder, so it can be used for sex and sexual activity. Actually, I really should point out that it doesn't just happen when aroused, it can happen at any time, especially when guys are going through puberty, and can be really embarrassing for them. Just like you may be unable to stop a period leak and the embarrassment that can cause when people notice and laugh about it, so too can an unwanted erection cause all sorts of embarrassment for guys. Don't be a bitch and laugh and make fun. Seriously. It's just rude.

I will also point out that there is very little correlation between how big a penis is when it is soft, to how big it will be when it is hard. Some penises can look tiny when flaccid and grow into monsters when hard, and others can look rather large when soft, but not change much at all when hard, and all the combinations of the two.

When an erect penis is stimulated it usually results in a male orgasm and ejaculation. That is basically the same thing as your orgasm except that a big spurt of liquid called semen comes out of the end of it. Semen is the liquid that contains sperm, which is the stuff that, when connected with your ovum (eggs) makes you pregnant. Semen can also carry diseases and infection and so, even if you're on the pill and are protected against pregnancy, you can still catch all sorts of STIs and get really sick. It's not worth it. ALWAYS USE A CONDOM!! And be aware that condoms don't stop you from getting certain diseases either. Check the chapter on STIs to get armed with all the info you need, and later on, in the Body Care section there is all kinds of information on sexual health, as well as instructions on how to put on, and use, a condom safely!

Orgasm and Arousal

Arousal is the heightening of your body's awareness to sexual stimulation. It is everything from flushed cheeks to a throbbing clitoris and all the heart-racing, skin-tingling sensations in between. It is your body and mind's way of preparing you for sexual enjoyment, and it can be incredibly overpowering and overwhelming. Sometimes when you get that feeling it is all you can do to stop yourself from hiding away to release that tension and bring it to climax by way of an orgasm.

So what is an orgasm?

The simplest way to describe it is like having a sneeze in your vagina. Okay, that sounds dumb I know, but it is. It's actually a very similar sensation and release and some people even say a sneeze is one eighth of an orgasm. That doesn't mean if you sneeze eight times you'll have an orgasm, it means for some people the intensity of the build up and the relief of an orgasm is about eight times more satisfying than the release of a sneeze. This is really only a guesstimate, though. Like with everything to do with "you," it is different for each person.

How does it happen? Well, like with a sneeze, the nerve endings in your clitoris, vagina, anus or nipples are stimulated like an itch, but unlike an itch being instantly cured by a scratch, the build up is not only part of the enjoyment, it also varies how long, and how intense it is before you climax. It can take anything from approximately sixty seconds, to over an hour, and in saying that, the time it takes to build up doesn't necessarily mean the climax will be greater or less than any other.

— *"The first time I had an actual orgasm I think I was about ten. I'd always played and enjoyed it but this was different. It actually built up and up and I couldn't stop. It was so weird. After I came I spent about half an hour laughing. My whole body felt like it was being tickled. After that I did it almost every time I could."* — Leigh, 17

— *"When I was about eleven I heard my older sister (eighteen) shouting and stuff in her room. I thought she was being hurt so I ran in there and saw her boyfriend with his head between her legs. I had no idea what was going on. I started to cry. I thought he was eating her. My sister had to sit me down and explain what was going on. She explained it really well so I wasn't scared any more. She also made me promise not to tell our mum. She taught me everything about sex and the feelings that go with it. I'm glad I had her. My mum wouldn't even talk about periods!"* — Geraldine, 17

Sciencey Stuff.

What happens when you get turned on?

The horny or toey feeling I mentioned before is the direct result of blood rushing to your vagina. Like how a guy gets a hard-on as a result of blood rush, so too does your vagina change and grow. The vagina becomes lubricated (wet), the outer lips swell and the clitoris grows and becomes hard. In internet land this has become known as a lady-boner and it really is like a little erection.

As the blood rushes, your breathing gets more shallow, your nipples harden and get more sensitive and, although the inside of your vagina increases in size (to let a penis fit in there), the opening itself becomes tighter (to hold the penis inside).

— *"I can literally feel my clit grow when I get horny. It becomes like this hard little nub thing. I once looked in a mirror and I couldn't believe how different it looked!" — Leigh, 17*

— *"[The first time I got wet] I thought I had wet myself! It soaked through to my jeans! I was so embarrassed! My boyfriend thought it was funny. I have learnt it's so much better than being dry though. That shit hurts!" — Cate, 18*

— *"If I am horny and someone touches my nipples I go crazy! It's like an electric shock. I actually punched someone once!" — Mary, 16*

What happens when you orgasm?

As you begin to orgasm your uterus, vagina, anus, thighs and stomach muscles all contract which can lead to involuntary spasms, noises and facial expressions. The more intense the orgasm, the stronger these things can be. Sex face, grunts, shakes, moans, the works. It can actually take more of an effort not to do these things than just to let go and allow them to happen. It's honestly nothing to be ashamed of. But I do know they can be embarrassing and I understand that sometimes other teenagers can be mean and cruel. It sucks.

When I was about fourteen I was with this guy, he was kissing me and touching me and it felt so good I asked him to move his fingers harder and faster. He did, and I orgasmed and it was awesome. Until the next day at school. I got there and all the girls were snickering at me and the boys too. I walked past a group of them and they all started whispering, "harder, faster!" at me. It was completely embarrassing and I felt absolutely betrayed by this boy. The solution was simply that I never went near him again. No matter how much he called and begged and came round to my house. He actually contacted me many years later and apologised, saying he had never felt so rotten and mean in his whole life and that he hadn't really known how to act or behave.

I'm not telling you this to scare you off expressing yourself, I am telling you because I want you to know that sex, sexuality and everything that comes with it is a learning curve and, especially in high school, can be a battleground of gossip and meanness. But that's high school. Kids are teased 'cause they aren't wearing the latest style jeans or don't watch the cool TV show that's all the rage, it's how it goes, but I promise you it doesn't last and it's also not always the case.

Another boyfriend I had, not long after that awful betrayer, once asked me why I was so quiet when we played. Why I wouldn't move or make any noise (which was bloody tricky to do I tell you). I explained to him what had happened and he was mortified for me. He showed me not all teenage boys are the same. That some really aren't dickheads without any respect. He helped me regain the confidence to express myself and, although our affair was pretty short-lived (a brief summer holiday fling), I never forgot the boost he gave me by making me feel normal. Which I was.

— *"I can't not make noise when I am orgasming. It's like this wave comes over me and I lose control. My best friend told the whole school I had been fingering myself at her house one day and I didn't hear the end of it til I left that school. She's not my best friend anymore."* — *Samantha, 17*

— "I don't care what anyone says. If I'm gonna come loudly then I'm gonna come loudly. Fuck them. Fuck them all. It's my enjoyment, not theirs!" — Kimberly, 17

— "I'm embarrassed of the noises I make. I know they aren't slutty or bad, but I can't help feeling like they are. I wish I could just let go." — Jess, 15

You can have from around three spasms up to over ten, depending on the intensity of the orgasm and, unlike men; there can often be no downtime between them so you can experience something completely unique to the human female which is multiple orgasms. This is basically building and climaxing several times in a row, either from just that single orgasm or from re-stimulating straight after and, I can tell you from experience, they are one of the most awesome things you will ever physically feel. It's like a running, looping, spiralling orgasm that just keeps on going. You know in those books and magazines where they talk about *toe-curling and spine-tingling*, well that's pretty much what happens. That's because the spasms run all the way down your legs and make your toes flex and, because the clitoris goes all the way from your vagina to your spine, it just continues up the nerves in your backbone and makes your whole body feel like jelly. It's bloody awesome.

NB see illustrations on next page

I read something once where a psychologist claimed the reason high heels were so sexy was because they put the feet in the same position they go in an orgasm. I'm a bit crap at walking in heels so I don't really know if that's the case, but the theory is kind of interesting.

Don't worry if you haven't had a multiple orgasm. I didn't til I was in my twenties. Like all good things they must be practised and perfected and, in the next section, I'm going to help you learn to do it.

Brain Sex

There is one other really important organ your body needs in order to orgasm and that is your brain. Just like with any feeling and sensation, it is the messages the nerve endings send to the brain and how the brain receives it that is how we can feel and respond to the sensations.

Every part of your genitals is full of nerves, and, apart from the vagus nerve, they all flow back to the spinal column, which then shoots it up to the brain. Each of these nerves is different though, so a clitoral orgasm can feel a lot different from a vaginal orgasm, in the same way a tickle in your throat is different to a tickle in your nose.

The different nerves and their functions:

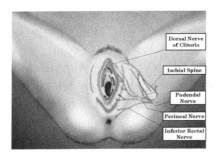 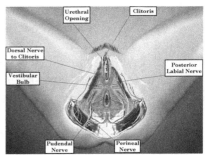

Hypogastric Nerve – sends messages to the spinal column from the uterus and the cervix

Pelvic Nerve – sends sensations from the vagina, cervix and rectum

Pudendal Nerve – are the nerves (over 8000 of them) in the clitoris

Vagus Nerve – comes from the cervix, uterus and vagina

But it's not just nerves and what they send to the brain that makes orgasms possible. It's also the way we think and feel about it too. The brain/mind is a very powerful tool. Think of those people who can stick sharp swords into their faces without flinching or bleeding, or people walking over hot coals. Sex can work the same way. If you are busy and distracted and stressed out it can be a lot harder to reach that climax, but if you're relaxed and happy it's a lot easier.

Being turned on is the same; being visually or mentally stimulated, like from watching or reading something sexy, can be the fastest and surest way to get to that awesome peak, just as something off-putting can make you completely uninterested in getting there.

Getting Turned On

Probably the best and quickest way to get yourself turned on is to read or watch something sexy. For most girls (but certainly not all and by no means the "only right way") it is through mental stimulation. Reading a sexy story or imagining a scenario in your head, because most porno magazines and things like that are restricted to over 18s. Probably the best things you can get for that quick fix of horny is erotic books which have no age restrictions on them and cover a wide range of themes from virgin brides to hardcore bondage and discipline. Erotic literature has come a long way in the past twenty years and laughable phrases like "throbbing manhood" and "silky thighs" have moved into more modern terms and settings. It really doesn't have to be explicit stuff either. I remember there was a movie I saw once when I was about 14. It was just a normal movie with a sex scene in it, I actually don't even think there were boobs, but the kissing in it was so appealing to me, sometimes that was all I needed to imagine in my head when I masturbated to get turned on and make myself orgasm. Other kissing scenes in movies didn't really have that effect but it's always stuck with me. And, even now, when I kiss someone who kisses like they did in that movie, I get delicious tingles throughout my whole body.

Arousal really is an individual thing and it is also constantly changing. What turns you on, may not turn someone else on and, what turned you on last week might not work the week after. Also the hormone levels in your body can change the frequency and strength of your sex drive. For example, most women are at their most horny in the week or so leading up to their period. This is because your body is in the process of getting ready to conceive, ovulation occurs (which is the releasing of the egg from the ovaries), and your hormones fluctuate to help the process. This often presents itself in horniness and the desire to have sex, because your body is preparing itself to get pregnant. Surprisingly a few other changes can happen to your body in those times. Actual physical changes. Your face and boobs align to become more symmetrical, your skin and eyes become brighter and your pheromones smell stronger. This is all in aid of attracting a mate. So just be super careful on those days. Your body and hormones can make you more inclined to do things you may not normally do, and think about things you may not normally think about and can act like a bit of a barrier to things like common sense and risk assessment.

Of course, this is all subjective and individual and everyone is different, but just be aware that, in the same way as your period can affect your mood in a negative way, ovulation and the lead up to your period can effect it in a more sexual way.

Bigger, Better, Stronger Orgasms

Orgasms are awesome, but did you know you can train your body to have even stronger, more intense ones? Yes! You really can. And it's actually quite simple. You see, just like anything you do, the more you practice the better you get and the more you can get out of it. If you play a musical instrument and practice every day and learn new techniques and new skills you get better and better to the point where you can start making up your own music and playing pieces that once looked like impossible tasks. Well, your body is your instrument and the more you play the better it gets! You learn which bits feel the best and where precisely on your body you like to be touched and, as you go on, you learn to find new bits and ways of touching that enhance all the other things.

One thing that can really help make orgasms more intense is a practice called edging. It's not complicated at all, but it can be a little tricky sometimes, although probably not in the way you're thinking. There are no special tools or positions or anything like that, but... Well, let me explain.

As I've talked about, orgasms are like a sneeze. There's the "Ah Ah Ah" (the build up) and then there's the "Choo" (the climax). Well, with edging, you don't allow yourself (at first) to get to the "Choo". Let yourself build up. Get as close as you can to the end and then, at the very last minute, stop. That can be the tricky bit. Sometimes an orgasm just takes over and there's no stopping it, and other times it just feels so good you don't want to stop. But if you can, stop before the climax and catch your breath. Let your body relax, let your heart-rate slow down and your tingling settle. Then, do it again... And stop. And again. You'll probably find each time it takes less and less time to reach your peak and then, when you can stand it no longer, let yourself come. It can seriously be the most intense, rolling orgasm you can have. Then (and this can be where toys come in handy) see if after that orgasm you can just keep playing to try and reach the peak again. You may find your body is just too sensitive and shivery and that's cool too.

But if you try, you never know, you just might be able to reach the peak again and again and again in that gorgeous multiple orgasm I mentioned earlier. It can take a while to perfect, and it might not happen every time you do it, but really, when you think about it, unlike practising your times-tables over and over, it's not a bad way to spend your time learning something.

G-spot orgasms can take a lot longer to perfect, and can be a bit harder to work out and, to be honest, can be rather exhausting at times. But they are definitely worth the work. These are achieved by pushing on the G-spot inside your vagina, usually quite hard and quite rapidly. The easiest way to explain how to do it is to put a couple of fingers inside your vagina and kind of curl or hook them towards where your belly button is. The skin there is slightly tougher and sometimes there's a little ridge, but each vagina is different so just play around a bit and see what you can find. You do need a little bit of pressure and you may well feel like you need to wee, but if you can push past this feeling and keep going, you can achieve an orgasm that may seem to take over your whole body. This is the sort of orgasm where most girls who squirt will squirt from. There are some really good sex toys out there that sort of curl over at the top which are specifically designed to stimulate your G-spot. Some girls also need clitoral stimulation to help bring it on, which is where the rabbit type vibrators can be useful.

It's a matter of experimenting and playing and getting to know your own body as well as you can to really get the best, deliciousness out of every orgasm you can.

What the Hell is Squirting?

Squirting for the most part is a learned thing although some girls are able to do it easily and without much effort at all. Basically it's a large gush or squirt of liquid which is unlike any other fluid your vagina produces. It comes from the female prostate gland and, even though it comes from the urethra (where you wee from), it is not wee. Sometimes the smallest bit of urine can get mixed up with it but it is a lot clearer and less smelly than wee. There can also be a hell of a lot of it and can completely dehydrate you so the best thing to do, before you attempt to find and play with your G-spot, is lay a lot of towels down and make sure your bladder is empty. Drink lots of water, and have some handy for afterwards. Not all G-spot orgasms come with squirting, but nearly all of them are super-intense.

G-spot orgasms have been described as primal. You know how I mentioned before about noises and faces and spasms being rather hard to control anyway... A G-spot orgasm can make them virtually impossible to avoid.

— *"My BFF and I used to finger ourselves all the time when we had sleepovers. One time I was doing it and this massive spurt of stuff came shooting right out onto my hand! We both thought she had wee-d everywhere but it didn't smell like wee at all. It was so weird. And the noise she made! Whoa! I thought we would wake her parents for sure"* — *Jane, 17*

— *"I have heard of squirting. It sounds like fun! But I also heard it makes you wee. That doesn't sound too fun at all"* — *Leigh, 17*

Even though most of the orgasm nerves travel up the spine to the brain, some people who have become paralysed by having their spinal cord cut are still able to do it! Scientists still haven't figured out how!

A male pig can ejaculate for longer than half an hour!

When you orgasm, you release a chemical called oxytocin which has been clinically proven to help with bonding and relationship building, feelings of well-being and also pain relief! Masturbating during your period can relive cramps and some psychologists even say just thinking about sex can relieve pain.

Babies (both male and female) in-utero (in the womb) have been seen on ultrasound doing what looks like masturbation.

Masturbation

Masturbation. Fingering. Flicking the Bean. Wanking. Fapping. Double-Clicking the Mouse. Rubbing one Out. Self-Love. Having a Fiddle. Muff Manipulation. Driving the Pink Canoe. Playing with the man in the boat. Taco Tangoing. Strumming the Banjo. Spelunking. Jilling Off. Rubbin' the Nubbin.

Masturbation is the act of touching yourself to achieve sexual pleasure. Usually it is done by rubbing the clitoris but there are other ways too, like using your fingers (or other objects) to touch inside your vagina or anus, and some people can even reach orgasm just by having their nipples touched! Everyone is different and every way you touch yourself is normal. In fact, you've probably been masturbating and achieving some sense of pleasure from your body since you were a baby. When I say pleasure in that sense I don't mean sexual pleasure. Babies and kids have no concept of sex or sexuality really. They have a sense of sensation though, about what feels nice. It's why little boys are always tugging at themselves and why little girls will often touch themselves without any kind of embarrassment. And really, that's because it's *not* embarrassing. It's normal. It's other people who put those terms on kids and it's wrong. It's really only when we grow up and begin to reach and go through puberty that we look at those feelings as sexual, but even then, it's still more about the feeling, the tickle, and the end release.

Let me stress, it does not make you weird or perverted. It does not make you some sort of sexual deviant freak. It just makes you like every other teenage girl (and boy) in the world.

It is time to start thinking about your vagina in positive ways. Good ways. It is not an embarrassing part of your body. No more than your nose or your elbow is an embarrassing body bit. The more you learn to touch and love and appreciate the awesome feelings and things it can do, the more in touch with yourself you will become. I know, it can be a bit tricky to push all those embarrassing feelings aside, especially if you have been told all your life it's wrong and dirty; but it is a bit like working a muscle or learning to read. The more you do it, the easier it becomes. Simply put, it's a big load of bullshit how it's frowned upon by people and also how a lot of the time it's deemed acceptable and almost encouraged for boys to have a tug, but for girls it's all dirty and wrong. Screw that with a big fuck off. Seriously. If you want to fiddle, go ahead and fiddle. Okay, so it's probably best not to do it on the bus or on the school oval, but in the privacy of your own bedroom or bathroom it is perfectly okay.

No matter what your mum or grandmother or other people say, masturbation is completely normal. It won't send you blind. It won't ruin your vagina. It won't send you to hell. It won't damage you for future men or women. It's just like scratching an itch. And, like an itch, sometimes it's so unbearable to ignore you just have to go rub one out. This feeling is called being horny or toey. It's a feeling (usually) in your vagina and low in your belly that's a bit like a tickle and, if you touch yourself, or sometimes even just cross your legs, the feeling intensifies. Quite often the feeling comes when you're watching, reading or doing something a bit sexy, but there are also times when the feeling will just hit you, out of the blue, for no reason at all.

— *"I was in Maths and we were doing algebra. So not sexy or anything. And suddenly, like right out of nothing, I was horny. I kept crossing and uncrossing my legs and I felt really sweaty. It was crazy. I don't know where it came from. I eventually went to the toilet and played with myself. It was a relief. I was sure everyone would know, but no-one said a thing. And if you know the girls at my school, if they HAD known, I wouldn't have heard the end of it"* — Kathy, **16**

— *"I was about twelve when I found my older brother's porno magazine collection. It was the stories in the letters section that got me going. I would hide under my covers with a torch and read them and then would masturbate until I orgasmed. I never told anyone, but my mum found the magazines and told me I was going to hell. Lucky I didn't believe her. I've been doing it ever since"* — Mary, **16**

— *"Oh my god, I love flicking the bean. If I have a test or an assignment due it's what I do to relax and get my mind focussed. It's so good. I can't wait for HSC."* — Kimberly, **17**

Losing It –
The Big V

Before we go on to this chapter, I need to make something very clear to you. Virginity, the "Big V" is a myth. There really is no such thing. This idea that you're "different" after losing your virginity comes from the same idea that girls who have sex are wrong and dirty. This odd idea that virginity is some sort of a special gift you can give to someone, or that girls who have lost it are not as "good" or "pure" as someone who hasn't is ridiculous and offensive.

First of all we need to examine what even IS virginity and losing it? If it's classed as PIV (Penis in Vagina sex) then there are a million lesbian virgins out there who would argue to the core that they are not virgins. If it is the breaking of the hymen then there are a million girls out there who have never had sex ever who would be classed as non virgins. Let me also just say, the idea that the hymen itself is some sort of purity seal is untrue and ridiculous. Firstly the hymen is never a fully sealed membrane. Well, no, it can be, but it is rare and can lead to all sorts of complications with things like periods and healthy discharge and vaginal function. Secondly it is so easily broken doing something as simple as riding a bike or dancing that

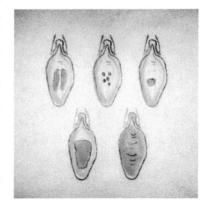

using it as a litmus test for "purity" is just dumb. And thirdly, no hymen is the same. Have a look at the diagram here. These are just some examples of what a healthy hymen looks like.

With all the knowledge we have today on sex, sexuality and sexual practices, the idea of virginity is an old-fashioned and completely unscientific theory that is pretty much only there to tell girls how to be "good" and to control those we deem "bad."

The whole concept of "losing" something is twisted and backwards and is associated with negativity. It's not a loss at all. It's a step. A step in your life that leads to a whole new world. It's a gain in knowledge. A gain in learning about your body. A gain in experience. You are not "losing your innocence," you are not "damaged goods." You are a person who had sex for the first time. That's it. You are still the same person. You've just reached another step in your journey to adulthood.

Now, let's look at the first time we have sex, and what that actually means.

If you haven't already realised it, I love sex. It is exciting, funny, energising and good for you. It's good for your insides and outsides and for your physical and mental well being. It is one of my favourite past times, stress relievers and ways to express myself. I love it so much I have made an entire life and career out of it.

Just to clarify and ease the minds of those who are starting to feel overwhelmed, to enjoy sex and be good at it you don't have to be a "sexpert" like me. I'm definitely a bit outside the box when it comes to sex and sexual enjoyments, but I know my stuff, I know other people's stuff and I want to help you figure out your stuff. I want you to enjoy sex, and get the very best out of it that you can and help you discover what works for you in exactly the right ways.

I know many of you will have been told all the horrors about sex. The diseases, the unplanned babies, the emotional head-fucks, all of it, and I will too because they are important and necessary facts to know about sex, but I will also tell you all the super awesome best things that can come from sex because there are a ton of those too.

The thing about sex is, it comes with a hell of a lot of responsibility and the only way to get the best, and avoid the worst, of it is to arm yourself with as much knowledge and information as you can. The good, the bad and the ugly. And when I say ugly, I mean it. I'm not trying to scare you, but I am going to arm you with as much information as possible. Only then can you truly enjoy and understand the awesomeness that is sex, and properly protect yourself from the bad.

When you do it properly and for the right reasons, sex will be one of the most enjoyable things you will ever do. It connects you to the person you're having sex with and, more importantly, it connects you with yourself.

If you don't do it for the right reasons, however, sex really can fuck you up. Pretty badly. And, unfortunately, it's a hell of a lot easier to do it the wrong way, than it is to do it the right way, and by wrong way, I'm not talking about positions, I'm talking about the reasons you do it.

Reasons NOT To Have Sex:

— He wants to but you're not sure.

— You think it will make him like/love you more

— All your friends are doing it

— You've been dating X amount of time

— You think it will make you popular/fit in

— You've already gone *this* far, it's not fair to back out now

Reasons TO have sex:

— You want to (and the person you want to have sex with wants to as well)

The above rules apply to everyone. Absolutely everyone. You. Me. Everyone. Regardless of how many times you have had sex before, and with however many people.

As I mentioned in the beginning of this section, sex can be good (really, really good), it can be bad, and it can be ugly (really, really ugly). All sex has the potential to be any of them so let's go step by step through it to make sure you only experience the most positive outcomes, and where better place to start than at the beginning: Losing your virginity. It is a pretty major decision in your life and doing it at the wrong time and for the wrong reasons can potentially set you up for a confusing and damaging sex life in later years.

The thing about having penetrative sex for the first time is, and I'm going to be super blunt here, it's probably going to suck a bit. Or at least, it's not going to be anything like those Vaseline-lensed, steamy erotic encounters you see on the TV. It's most likely not going to be breathless and orgasmic and, all that stuff about souls entwining and fireworks and passion — bullshit. Utter bullshit. The real hard fact is it's probably going to be rather uncomfortable, it might even hurt and make you bleed, and will most likely only last a minute or so. In fact, as much as it can be a huge milestone leap in your growth and development as a sexual person, and as much as it is an exciting concept and an adventure in exploration, the expectations of what your first time will be like is probably one of the most overrated things you'll ever come across.

Honestly, no matter how many tampons you've used, or how much you've masturbated, I can almost 100% guarantee you the first time (and probably the next few times) you have sex will be a bit of a letdown. Now before you go writing me angry Facebook posts about how excellent your first time was, let me just say this. AWESOME!! You really are a rare exception and I am so happy for you that your first steps into sex were fantastic. You can pretty much only go up from here! But overall, the first few times you do it will be awkward and fumbly and a bit funny.

Okay, yes, making the decision to have sex for the first time is a pretty big thing. It can be seriously life changing and you will probably feel different afterwards, but not necessarily in the way you think. Some people can feel euphoric and ecstatic, other people can feel empty and isolated, and all the emotions and feelings in between those two. It's also important to understand that NOT feeling any of those things is perfectly normal and okay too, because that's the thing. We are all different and process things differently. How your best friend felt afterwards is not a guarantee that you will feel the same.

So, here's the kicker, how do you know when you're ready? Unfortunately, that's not something I can tell you in a book. No-one can. Only you will know when the time is right for you. The tricky thing can be sorting out in your own mind if you really are ready, or if you are doing it for one of the reasons stated above, so read them over, think about it like you've never thought about anything before and then read them over again.

Let's break them down a bit.

He wants to and you think it will make him like/love you more:

The sad fact is, some guys will say just about anything to get you to have sex with them. Not all guys let me be clear, but a lot of them. You see, in exactly the same way as most girls are conditioned to believe sex is shameful and dirty and not what "good girls" do until they are married or at least in a long term, loving relationship, most boys are conditioned to believe sex is a mark of pride, honour and manliness. The more chicks you can score, the more valid your man-card. It's a twisted logic and a dangerous combination of values that so often leads to low self esteem issues and other mentally damaging effects on both sides of the spectrum.

Because of this conditioning, girls are quite often hard-wired into associating sex with love and, because boys know this, they will often take advantage of it. Please do not be fooled! I'm not saying boys don't fall in love, and I'm not saying they will be lying when they tell you they love you. What I am saying is if the only reason you are having sex is because he told you he loves you and you think it will make him love you more, or not leave you, or not like another girl more, then you are kidding yourself. If you do not want to have sex, if you are not ready to, or not in the mood, or any other reason whatsoever and he really does love you, then you not having sex should not be an issue at all. Because love is essentially about trust and respect and he needs to respect your decision. That is proof of love.

— *"My boyfriend told me he would break up with me if we didn't do it. We'd been going out for about six months. I really didn't want him to dump me so I did it. It was horrible. I cried after and he went to play footy. Then he dumped me the next week anyway. I felt like a dickhead." — Lucy, 16*

— *"Me and my friend decided we wanted to have sex. It was really just a random thing. It was okay I guess." — Penny, 15*

— *"I dumped a guy 'cause he wouldn't stop asking me to have sex. I didn't want to lose him, but I didn't want to have sex either. He went and told all his friends he dumped me 'cause I was a bad root. It was fucked! But in my own head I knew I was right" — Karen, 15*

— *"My boyfriend waited until I was ready. It hurt a bit and I felt weird afterwards, but we both did so that was okay" — Mary, 16*

All your friends are doing it and you want to fit in:

Peer pressure, mixed with the hormones and emotions from puberty and growing up can really confuse people and, to be honest, even once you're through all that and have become an adult it can still be a hard road to navigate.

When I talk about peer pressure, it doesn't even have to be as overt as "Don't you want to be as cool as us" or "If you have sex with me I will like you more," it can come in so many subtle forms that most of the time you don't even know you're being pressured.

Take what you see on TV for example. Music video clips are full of sex and sexual innuendo. Every pop star from Madonna to Beyonce has a way of saying, "Sex is really cool and you can be cool too if you do it." Whether it's the lyrics they sing or the visuals in the clip; sex and sexiness is probably the biggest seller and the strongest message given to teenagers (and everyone else) through popular culture.

The other side of the peer pressure coin is, of course, the pressure NOT to have sex because of the way you may be regarded by the people around you. The awful thing is, it is quite often other girls who are the worst. We are almost all guilty of it. My younger self included in that. I was brought up, (via school friends not my parents), with the idea that a girl wearing certain types of clothing is a slut, or a girl flirting with the boys is "asking for trouble" and if she has had sex she is probably distrustful and dirty and after your boyfriend. Admit it, you've thought that too haven't you? You've bitched about someone to your friends and have used the word "slut" or, on the opposite end, "frigid" to describe her. You've looked down your nose at someone who is, in your opinion, too sexual or not sexual enough and you've even gone so far as to speculate on someone's honesty and morals if they have reported a sexual assault. A lot of the time, you've probably done it without realising it and have most likely had it done to you.

— "At my school all the popular girls talk about having sex all the time. But if anyone else does it they call them a slut. I don't get it. I hate the girls at my school" — Kathy, 16

— "My best friend is a guy and all the popular girls used to call me a slut and spread rumours we were doing it. He was the only person who knew I was actually gay. It bothered me a lot at the time, now I just think 'Meh'" — Deb, 17

— *"When I was about 14 there was a girl in my class who apparently had sex with everyone. We were all so mean to her and called her a slut and a whore. I feel awful about it now."*
—Leigh, 17

— *"My best friend and I have a pact. When we do it, we won't tell anyone but each other. The girls at our school are bitches."*— Susan, 14

You've been dating for this long, or have gone this far, it wouldn't be fair on them to stop now or say no:

The minute someone does not respect your boundaries and pushes you further than you want, or makes you do something you don't want to do and makes you uncomfortable, then the act itself becomes one of sexual assault. Whether it is an unwanted hug or grope, or a kiss, or in the worst cases, penetration. If you have said no and asked them to stop, and they haven't, it is sexual assault. It doesn't matter if you have spent the last hour kissing and touching, if you tell someone to stop and they don't, it is sexual assault. It doesn't matter if you are smiling and flirting and wearing a short skirt, if someone touches you when you do not want them to, *it is sexual assault.* Anything other than mutual consent between the people involved *is sexual assault.*

Don't let phrases like "cock teaser" and "you lead him on" make you question your choice; these are phrases that have been created to add to the female oriented shame of having sex. You're bad when you do, and bad when you don't. Don't listen to it. All it is going to do is make you feel ashamed and somehow in the wrong no matter what decision you end up making.

Sexual assault is more common than you probably think. One in three women will be assaulted sexually in their lifetimes. So, if you look at just the female members of your family it's probably a pretty safe bet at least one of them has been (or will be) raped or assaulted in some way or another. It's a terrifying statistic and, when you think about the number of women who don't report it, the number probably doubles.

One of the most important things we can do to change these statistics is to not be ashamed to speak up when it happens. No matter what anyone says or accuses you of, it is never your fault when someone decides to take without permission. Never. No matter what you were wearing, what you were talking about, how many people you have slept with before, how much you have had to drink or what you may have been doing five minutes previously. Think about it this way, you would never accuse someone of "asking to be robbed" because they wear a nice suit and drive a fancy car; no-one ever "asks to be raped" no matter what the circumstances of their life or personality might be.

— *"I was with this boy. He was getting really into it but I told him I wasn't sure if we should keep going but he said it would be fine. I didn't know what to do. We ended up having sex and I think I cried for a week afterwards. I think I was raped, but I never said no so maybe I wasn't." — Jess, 15*

— *"My boyfriend and I play together a lot. We usually make each other come. But I have told him I don't want to have real sex yet. He's cool with that. He doesn't even ask me anymore. He knows when I want to I will tell him." — Bec, 16*

— *"I was at a party and this guy kept grabbing me on the boobs and bum. I told him to stop. He wouldn't. One of my male friends punched him and called him a rapist. The guy called me a slut and a fight broke out. I felt like it was all my fault but I was so glad my friend helped me." — Karen, 15*

Okay, so you've read through the list, you've thought about it and you've decided you're ready. Now, how do you go about it?

If you are in a relationship, or you know who you're ready to have sex with, the first thing you need to do is talk to them. Any relationship, whether sexual or platonic, thrives on communication, trust and respect so be open and honest in your talks. Part of being ready to have sex, is being ready to talk about sex and if you can't talk openly to your partner about your wants, needs and concerns, maybe you need to read over the list at the top of the page again.

When I say talk about your wants, needs and concerns I mean things like:

- Where and when do you want to have sex?

- What will make you feel the most comfortable

- What is exciting you about it?

- What is scaring you about it?

- What do you really want to try?

- What do you not want to do?

- Who will you (or they) tell?

That is just a basic list of things and with each one you ask another hundred will pop up, but it's a great starting block to a healthy and communicative sex life. It's really important that you and your partner are on the same page otherwise something along the way may go horribly wrong.

The final question there, the one about telling people, is a huge one. I truly believe having someone to talk to apart from your partner is really important; however I also believe you have to choose the right person. Sometimes teenage friendships can be fickle and what is told in confidence one day is texted to everyone in your class, or written all over Facebook and Tumblr and every other social media site you can think of. That's not to say don't trust your friends, but just be aware some people are not what they seem and can cause a lot of trouble in the name of jealousy, bitchiness and popularity.

Some people find they really need to be in love to have sex and other people aren't too fussed about the emotional side of it. Both are completely normal and, as stated so many times in this book, there are no right or wrong ways, just YOUR way. I also need to point out not all people who find themselves ready to have sex are in a relationship. That's okay too. You don't have to be. The ground can be a little trickier to navigate in this situation, especially when you've never done it before, but it's not impossible, and is just as exciting and important an event in your life as anyone else's.

The open communication with the person you're going to have sex with may be a bit harder in this case (especially if you don't know who you want to have sex with yet, just that you want to) but I think it is really important to let someone know what you are about to do, and also tell the person you're about to sleep with you are a virgin. If they have had sex before they will (hopefully) be gentle, patient and understanding. If they are not, and you feel in any way uncomfortable or pressured or unsafe, stop what you are doing *immediately*. This goes for any person of any age and circumstance, relationship or not. Saying no is your right and you can exercise that right at **any time**.

The main things to think about and remember in this (and indeed every) situation is your own personal safety and boundaries and to be aware of where you are and who you are with. Remember alcohol and drugs, apart from being illegal when you're under 18 (or taking any illicit drugs at any age), can really impair your decision-making skills. This is by no means telling you that if you're drunk you're going to invite bad things to happen, I don't believe anyone ever "invites bad things" to happen to them, but in the same way as you should never drive a car or rock climb or spend lots of money on a pair of really-awesome-I-have-to-have-them-right-now shoes when you're not in a sober state of mind, having sex is another one of those important things you should be in complete control of your mind when you do, especially if you are with someone you don't know all that well.

If you do happen to be with someone you don't know very well it is super important you let someone know where you are and who you are with and what you may possibly be going to do. Check out the "care call" box in this section for tips on how to keep yourself and your friends safe. Trust and communication are very important factors in any sexual situation and it is really, really hard to trust someone you don't know.

In the same way I have previously mentioned, it is really important to look out for your friends. If you think your friend

Care Call

- Keeping you and your friends safe!

- Let a friend know where you are going. Be as specific as possible with a venue or an address.

- Who are you going to be with? If you're meeting someone for the first time, give your friends the name and phone number of the person you are meeting up with.

- Are you drinking? Taking any substances?

- Arrange a meet-up time or a phone call/text time just to check in.

- Do you have a way to get home?

- It can be a good idea to work out a code word for if you are feeling unsafe. For example: If you say "everything is fine," then that's cool. If you say "everything is hunky dory," that's a code to your friend that you need help.

- Let the person/people you are with know you will be expecting a check up call/text.

is making a decision they would not normally make due to the influence of drugs or alcohol it is your responsibility to look out for them. This includes telling the person your friend is with that you are concerned about the state of mind your friend is in. Sure, they may both tell you to fuck off, but that shouldn't stop you from being concerned and alert and making sure that at least they are safe and using condoms. I cannot stress enough how important safety is when it comes to having sex. The safety of your body, as in contracting sexually transmitted infections and sexual assault; and the safety of your mind and thoughts, as in making sure you are making a decision that is right for you. No one but you has the right to make these choices for you, but remember, if a friend does pull you up on it, they are probably just worried about your safety. Just like the kid who steals their mum's car and goes for a joyride and ends up smashing into a tree and killing a friend, there are some choices we make that can be absolutely life changing and we all have a responsibility to look out for our friends and make sure everyone is safe.

Saying No

In all the discussions around sex and consent, in almost every article, book, blog, piece I read that talks about consent, I have always noticed one glaring gap.

Yes it is absolutely important to write about how only yes means yes, and your rights to say no whenever you feel like it, but has anyone ever taught you how to say no? I mean, it's all very well and good for me to say, "Hey girl, you don't have to do that thing, just say no," but it is an entirely different thing altogether to be in that situation with a person you really like and enjoy spending time with, to say no to them. It's not just peer pressure, it's the way we are with people we like. We don't want to disappoint them or let them down. We don't want to risk losing something or someone that we enjoy the company of. I'm not going to lie to you, saying no can be a whole lot harder than saying yes, although, in the long run, saying yes to something you don't want will probably linger with you far longer. But, to be blunt, as humans we are always more focused on the immediate rather than the long term. So even knowing that saying yes will stay with you longer than the no, in that immediate situation, the one where their hands are on you, and you're half naked and feeling kinda nice and completely unsure as to where you want to go in THAT moment ... yeah, that's tricky.

The main thing you will find is that saying no gets easier with practise, so it's a really good idea to start practising.

You can do this in a few different ways. The first is just to say it to yourself in the mirror.

Sounds dumb, I know, but it really can help! Stand in front of a mirror and say "no." Or "no I don't want to." Or other variations: "No, I'm not ready." "No, I don't feel comfortable."

The more you say it, the more comfortable the words will feel coming out.

Another helpful thing to remember is how to come back to a protest of your no. For example, you say no to your boyfriend and he says something like, "but if you loved me you would." It is perfectly okay to throw that back in their face: "If you loved me you wouldn't pressure me to do something I'm not comfortable with."

Emotional blackmail like that is a dangerous step towards abuse and it is really important to stay true to your convictions. It is okay to get up and walk away if you feel you are not being listened to. You are not in the wrong in that situation, or any situation you need to remove yourself from where you feel uncomfortable and not listened to.

Other comeback responses can be things like:

If they say: "But I thought you liked me," you can respond with something like, "I do like you, and I respect you. It would be nice if you respected me too."

If they say: "My balls will explode if we don't," you can reply with something like, "dude, go and read a biology book, they won't explode. If you're that worried, go and have a wank."

If they say something like, "but all our friends are doing it," you can come back with your mum's, "if everyone jumped off a bridge would you too?" comment, or something along the lines of, "why do you assume I will do something just because others do? I am my own person."

If they say something like, "We've done everything else, it's not that big a deal," then agree, that it isn't a big deal, and why are they so obsessed with it, and how much better it would be when you are both ready and both want it.

It is also okay to let them know that pushing you into it, that begging or pleading, that coercing and nudging. That all of that can be classed as sexual harassment and assault and if you want to appeal to their male ego, that it's not a cool look for a dude to have to beg for sex. Wouldn't they rather wait for someone who wanted to? And if not, are they really the sort of person you want to share your intimacy with?

Saying no to sex also doesn't mean you have to pack up your stuff and go home. I mean, if you're enjoying yourself and the situation but still don't feel ready to have intercourse (or any specific act) it's fine to let them know this without making them feel like you are rejecting all physical contact. Saying something like, "I am not ready to have sex, but can we do the thing with your fingers again?" or, "I really love the way you go down on me, let's just play like that together until we're both ready."

It's also important to note that being "ready" to have sex counts for every single time you have sex. Just because you were comfortable and wanted to do it yesterday, or with your last boyfriend/girlfriend, doesn't automatically mean you have to be ready to do it again the next time or with your next partner. Every single individual time you have sex you get to set the terms as to what you do or don't do with your body.

Remember:

It is okay to say no.

It is okay to say yes.

What is not okay is being forced or coerced into a decision you don't want to make.

The Nuts and Bolts of Sex

So now we've looked at all that sort of stuff, let's have a look at what sex actually is. Like what are the different sorts of sex and some of the terms and names for different things.

If you listen to basic biology, sex is the act of the penis entering the vagina but really, when you look at sex and sexuality and sexual pleasure, that's just one small part. I mean what about same sex couples who don't have one or the other of those body parts? Or sexual acts that have nothing to do with those body parts or at least the combination of penis in vagina. No, sex is a whole encompassing variety of things. Some you will enjoy and want to do and others that may have no interest to you whatsoever.

The following is a short list of sexual acts (and some, but by no means all, of the slang terms you may hear) that all come under the huge umbrella of sex. It is not a list of every sexual position out there, because that would be a ridiculously long book. In fact the Kama Sutra (an ancient Indian sex and sexuality guide) has over 60 different positions in it and even I haven't tried the majority of them so don't get too worried about doing it the "right way." If sex is consensual, there are no right or wrong ways to do it. It is all up to you and the person or people you are having sex with. (Please note I am using the examples of a male and female combination, but many of these sexual acts are also practised and enjoyed by same sex couples with the use of things like imagination, sex toys and other body parts).

Again, I need to stress, there should never be any pressure to perform any sexual act you do not feel comfortable doing. With all the stuff available on the internet in the form of porn and erotica, certain acts can be seen as "the norm" or "what everyone does." This is not true. For any of them. What is the norm for you could be completely different to what is the norm for someone else. Nothing should ever be expected of you. Nothing. It is entirely your choice, your right to decide, and up to you what you do or do not do.

Foreplay

In my opinion, foreplay is the most important part of sex. Foreplay is all the stuff you do leading up to having actual intercourse. It's everything from talking and kissing and touching and playing. It's flirting and sending sexy messages to each other. It is what gets you excited, in the mood, horny and wet. It can sometimes be even more fun than the actual sex itself. The lead up, the anticipation, the whole journey and experience.

Fingering and Hand Jobs

This is touching and playing with someone's genitals with your hand. It can be a really fun and sexy thing to do that can be mutually satisfying and just as exciting and sexy as having sex itself. Sometimes it can be a bit hard for someone to work out all your bits inside and outside of your vulva and vagina so it's perfectly okay to show them what it is you like. You can do this by telling them verbally, or non-verbally by showing what you like with your own hand or moving theirs to where you like it. A combination of the two is the best way to get your message across. If it hurts or scratches (fingernails can be a bit of an issue sometimes, so always remember to keep yours trimmed and non-jagged) then it's super important to speak up. Lube can also help with hand jobs or wanking someone. It makes things slippery and fun and can mimic actual sex in some ways. Latex gloves can also be a fun way to play. The lube will make them extra slippery, and it's a great way to play safely as the gloves are just like a condom for your hand. You may think that sounds silly, but even something little like a torn cuticle can be an entrance into your blood stream, so it's definitely a good idea to be safe.

Oral Sex

Giving head, going down, 69ing.

Oral sex is the act of pleasuring someone's genitals with your mouth. This can also be areally sexy thing to do and enjoy, as well as so much fun. You should never feel pressured into giving or receiving it and, just like with any sexual act, it should be a mutually enjoyable thing. If it makes you uncomfortable or hurts or makes you feel bad in any way you should stop doing it.

Oral Sex on a guy – Fellatio.

Going down, giving head, blowjob/blowie, giving a gobbie, sucking off, hummer/humming.

Although it is called a "blow job," you do not actually blow onto or into the penis, but use your mouth to suck and lick it. There are a few schools of thought as to why it is called a "blow job." The most common ones being that it's short for "below job," or because an old fashioned term for ejaculation was "blowing." You may have even heard people say, "I'm gonna blow my load," or other similar sentiments. There's also the idea it's called that because it looks like you're "blowing a horn," and another thought is it comes from old fashioned term for sex workers, "blowsies." But really, it doesn't matter where the word comes from, just remember not to blow.

When giving head, you can also incorporate the testicles (balls), and use your hands at the same time too. It can be done slow or fast or however you want to do it. It is not the act of just opening your mouth and letting a guy ram his penis down your throat (unless, of course that is something you enjoy and want to do) and there is no right or wrong way to do it. Everyone enjoys different things and different techniques so it's really up to you and the person you are with to determine what feels best and what is mutually enjoyable.

As stated above you should never feel pressured to do it, and if you are not enjoying it you have every right to stop. Being forced by someone holding your head down and not respecting your wishes is sexual assault. You should always use a condom because some STIs can be transmitted through oral sex. If you do not use a condom, having someone ejaculate (come) into your mouth is absolutely your choice. If you do not want this to happen then you need to tell them to stop and pull out before they come. Not listening to your wishes and disrespecting your choices is sexual assault.

As a little aside, it's probably a good idea not to use your teeth, unless specifically asked to do so.

Oral Sex on a girl – Cunnilingus

Going down, eating out, growling out, licking out, eating at the Y, carpet munching.

This is when someone uses their mouth to pleasure your vagina. It feels a lot different to having someone use their fingers or having sex and can create some really unique and pleasurable sensations. Although not always the case, oral sex like this is usually concentrated on the clitoris and outside parts of your vagina, although again, like with giving head to a guy, there is no right or wrong way and it's great fun to figure out what feels the best for you.

A little tip I read many years ago, which I have used myself and have suggested to other people when they're a bit confused as to how it all works down there is to get them (or you if you are the one performing it) to use their tongue and gently trace the letters of the alphabet over your clitoris. Remember from the diagram of the vagina, the clitoris spreads out into the outer lips of the labia so licking and sucking on them can also feel pleasurable. Using fingers to play as well can also be a great way to get some awesome feelings out of it. There really should never be any teeth involved either as the skin folds are very sensitive and it should never be painful. If it hurts, makes you feel uncomfortable or you just don't want to do it, then you have every right to stop.

69ing

This is where both people are giving oral sex to each other at the same time. It can be done with the guy on top, the girl on top or by lying side by side. It can be a bit of a feat trying to work it all out. Elbows and knees and hair and all sorts of things can get in the way, and it is important to make sure both people are comfortable and able to breathe properly, but it can be a really fun activity.

I've always found it a bit unfair that guys seem to expect a blowjob but are sometimes reluctant or weirded out by the thought of going down on a girl. In my opinion what is good for the goose is good for the gander and if they aren't going to do it to you, then they have no right to expect you to do it to them.

Intercourse

Having sex, fucking, banging, rooting, doing it, grinding, bumping uglies, bonking, humping, tapping, boning, getting it on, having nookie.

This is your "standard" definition of sex. It is the penis entering the vagina and, most often, moving it in and out. There are many different ways to have intercourse and depending on the position you do it in, there are often different sensations and enjoyment levels.

Some of the more common positions are as follows.

Missionary: This is when the male is on top and the

female is underneath. Although often referred to as boring and "samey," missionary is a really great position for intimacy. You are face to face with your partner so you can kiss and look at each other. You can really wrap your arms and legs around them so they are closer to you, and it's really not complicated and doesn't require you to be some sort of contortionist or gymnast to get into position and enjoy yourself.

Doggie Style: This is the position where the female is on all fours and the male enters her from behind. This position can allow the penis to enter in a slightly deeper way. It can be great for G-spot stimulation and can also allow for the clitoris to be played with at the same time (either by the female touching herself or the male in a reach around).

Cowgirl: This is where the male is on his back and the female sits on top facing the male. It's really good for allowing the female to control the pace and the depth of the penetration and, like missionary, allows for face to face contact. It also is good for clitoral play and boob play too.

Reverse Cowgirl: This is the same as the cowgirl position except for the fact that the female sits the other way round facing the male's feet. It again allows the female to have more control over the pace and the depth of penetration and can allow for clitoral and anal stimulation if you desire.

Anal Sex/Anal play: Anal sex and play is where a penis (or finger or sex toy) enters into the anus. It is an entirely different feeling to having vaginal sex and, for some people, can be quite painful and uncomfortable, especially to begin with (even more so than losing your virginity). The skin on the inside of the anus is very different to that of the vagina. It is nowhere near as flexible or stretchy or lubricated. If you are going to engage in anal sex always wear a condom (the skin inside the anus is likely to tear and bleed and catch infections very easily) and always, *always always* use lots of lube. Lots. Heaps. Drown yourself in it. Insert it inside the anal cavity too. Like heaps! Squirt away! You can never use "too much" lube when it comes to anal play! But seriously, anal sex can take a lot more getting used to than vaginal sex and is, like any sexual act, entirely up to you whether or not you want to engage in it.

What Are Erogenous Zones?

Erogenous zones are the bits on your body that, when touched, give you a sexy tingle. They can be different for everyone, they can change over time and they can also be more sensitive at different times of your menstrual cycle and even depending on what you are doing at the time. Some of the more common ones are lips, nipples, feet, necks, and thighs. But there are really no rules. If someone touching your hands makes you feel tingly, that's cool. If you get a buzz out of your belly being stroked that's perfectly normal too. Any part of your body has the ability to be an erogenous zone. It also doesn't mean that every time you touch it or it is touched it will have the same effect. Like for example, you may love having your lips touched, but putting lipstick on may not give you the same feeling or having a shoulder massage might be a completely different feeling to having someone touch them when you are feeling horny.

I also believe, when it comes to sex, ladies should come first. As in have an orgasm before the guy does. It is very rare (no matter what you see in movies or read in books) for both the male and female to orgasm at the same time, and often, once a guy has orgasmed, they can lose interest (not in you but in further sexual activity). This is because a male orgasm is a rather exhausting thing for a penis and they are mostly (unlike us lucky females) unable to come again for a while after they've ejaculated. So it is perfectly acceptable for you to make them wait until you have orgasmed before it is their turn. This really is a good way to ensure a mutually satisfying encounter for everyone.

Age Of Consent.

This refers to the legal age in which you are allowed to have sex. It varies from state to state and if you or the person you are with, is under the age of consent, and the other person is over the age of consent you or they can get into a heap of trouble. It is called statutory rape and depending on the age difference between the people having sex it can eventuate in charges and jail time.

That means until you are of the age of consent in your state or territory, you are not allowed to have sex with someone who is over that age. And even then, there are certain laws that mean someone a lot older than that (more than two years) or who is in a position of power over you (like a teacher or a guardian) may not have sex with you. There are serious consequences including up to ten years jail time for an offender.

The age of consent per state is as follows:	
VIC - 16	QLD – 16
ACT – 16	WA – 16
NSW – 16	TAS – 17
NT – 16	SA - 17

If both people involved are under the age of consent, and there are no major age gaps (for example, it would still be illegal and punishable if a fifteen year old has sex with a ten year old) or coercions or power plays (like, for example, if someone is intoxicated and unable to make coherent choices or is mentally disabled and unable to make informed decisions) then it is not illegal for them to have sex.

For a full look at all the laws and all the information that comes under these laws it is a good idea to have a look at the Australian Government website at the consent laws information page at

http://www.aifs.gov.au/cfca/pubs/factsheets/a142090/index.html

REMEMBER:

IT IS JUST AS OKAY TO BE A VIRGIN AS IT IS TO WANT TO HAVE SEX!!!!

THERE IS NOTHING WRONG WITH YOU IF YOU DON'T WANT TO HAVE SEX!!!

There is just as much "virgin" shaming in this world as there is "slut shaming" and it's ridiculous. Your sex life and your sexual experiences are your own business and no-one else's. It doesn't matter if you fuck every person you meet, or you never have sex your entire life ever. The only thing that matters is that it is your choice and your decision. Remember this in all ways. For all people. For all genders. Sex is personal. It is none of your damn business what someone else does or doesn't do with their genitals, as long as it is always consensual. You are not the "sex" police. Nor is anyone else. Live your way and let others live theirs. It's not rocket science.

Love and Lust
in the
Age of Technology

Love

Falling in love for the first (and the second and third etc.) time is awesome. It really is. It's an amazing bubbly, exciting, happy time. You start to notice how meaningful song lyrics are, how that band wrote that song just for you and how you feel about that special person. Romeo and Juliet have nothing on what you're feeling. It's like you could fly. Like you can see the future all smiley and sunshiny. It's totally fucked up how your parents will laugh at you and call it "puppy love" and tell you "you aren't really in love, you'll KNOW when you are." because you DO know. You absolutely 100% know you are in love and the world is made of diamonds and sparkles and nothing will ever be the same again. It's even more exciting and awesome and happy when the person you are in love with loves you back. The first relationship. The first kiss. The holding hands as you walk down the street. It is like you're invincible. You're going to be in love forever.

Lust

Lust is slightly different to love. Lust is mostly physical, although (to confuse things even more) it feels really similar to love and can be just as full of emotional ups and downs. When you are in lust with someone it's usually your body (specifically your genitals and other erogenous zones) that feels it. You want to touch them and be touched by them and your whole body is consumed by the thought of them (see, really similar to love). It is really, really hard to separate the two feelings of love and lust and, unfortunately, as you get older, it doesn't really get all that easier.

— *"When I look at him I feel it in my tummy"* — *Bec, 16*

— *"She just gets me. I don't have to say anything and she gets me"* — *Deb, 17*

— *"He actually has no idea I exist. But that doesn't stop me from following him home from school every day."* — *Jess, 15*

Heartbreak

Probably the main difference between love and lust is how you feel when it's all over, which, I'm sure you'll agree, is not the best way to find out anything.

Heartbreak is just awful. Seriously. One of the worst things you will ever go through, and something that, although may get less frequent as you grow up, doesn't stop being horrible. That gut wrenching, heart tightening, devastated feeling when the person you desire, the person you love, doesn't feel the same way about you anymore. It hurts. Physically, emotionally, every way. Your belly feels like a giant hole has formed in it, sucking everything into it like a black hole. Your chest feels heavy and sometimes even breathing hurts. You cry, oh god, you cry like you've never cried before and, if I am completely honest with you, you never really get over it. Not your first heartbreak. The first guy to break my heart was a guy I was going out with when I was fourteen/fifteen. We had been going out for around nine months (I know, right! That's like a marriage when you're fourteen) and then, one night, at a disco with all my friends, he dumped me. There wasn't really a reason given (although he started dating another girl almost immediately so I'm pretty sure I know why) and my whole world crumbled. I ached like I have never ached before. I couldn't sleep; I did nothing but cry and eat. Nothing mattered. Nothing but the hole in my being and the pain of loss I was sure was my soul being torn apart. I am well into adulthood now and still, when I think about it, over every other boyfriend and break up I have ever had, the memory of that particular heartache is the one I remember the clearest. I mean, I'm not in love with him anymore, I haven't been for over twenty years, but that pain of rejection, the first time you ever feel it, is a feeling that stays with you. You do learn from it, but you never forget it.

If someone does break your heart, one of the worst things you can do, both for yourself and for them, is to not accept it's over. Crying at them, begging them, sending them endless texts or phone calls, calling their friends, going over to their house, it's just not worth it. It will make you feel worse. It really, really will. When I was about 16 a guy broke up with me. We had been together over a year. He broke up with me because I caught him with another girl. I'd begged and pleaded for him to choose me. He didn't. I remember asking my mum to drive me over to his house. I figured all I had to do was see him and for him to see me and he would change his mind. He would love me again. I was convinced of it. My mum refused. Flat out refused. She told me it would hurt me more. It would make me feel like a fool. It would only make him scoff or ignore me further. I didn't believe her. What would she know? She was old and had obviously forgotten what it was like. I begged and cried and pleaded and swore. Finally she rolled her eyes and said, "Okay, you asked for it," and drove me over. You know what? She was right. Oh so right. He looked at me all red-faced and swollen eyed and weepy and you know what he did? He just shook his head. Told me he had said it was over and just walked away, back into his house and shut the door.

My mum was cool. She didn't say "I told you so" she didn't have to.

If someone breaks your heart, then give it time to heal. Eat chocolate. Listen to sad songs. Watch romantic movies and cry into your pillow. Bitch with your bestie. Buy a pair of shoes. Scream really loud and take up a boxing class. Go for a walk. Hug a puppy. Do something that will make you feel better, even if just for a short time. Because it *WILL* get better. It **WILL** stop aching in that horrible, horrible way I promise.

Don't date his best mate just to get back at him. Don't hurt yourself or threaten to just to try and win him back. Don't call his new girlfriend a slut or threaten to kick her head in (even if he cheated on you with her. Remember HE is the one who cheated, not her. If it happens to be your best friend he cheated with, and, oh god, THAT'S horrible, trust me I know, then she was never your friend to begin with. As much as it hurts, the above points about begging and pleading go for her too. Anyway, violence is NEVER the answer). Don't write mean things on Facebook. Don't send his personal messages and photos to all his friends. And, most importantly, don't let it make you forget just how awesome you really are. Because you are.

And if you DO do any of those things, just remember for every action there is a consequence and sometimes those consequences are just not worth it. Not for anyone. Not even the person you love.

And what about if you're the one who falls out of love. You want to break up with someone. You become the heart breaker. It's still not easy. The pain is still there, although not as intense because it usually doesn't come with the pain of rejection too, but it's still not easy.

When you do decide it's over and you want to break up with someone please be respectful of their feelings and their heartbreak because, no doubt, they will feel it like the above description and they will be, no doubt, doing all the same things and thinking all the same stuff. Don't break up with them over the phone, or in a text message or on a Facebook update. Seriously. That's callous and rude and just plain heartless. Yes, it is hard to tell someone it's over, but you owe it to them and to yourself to do it properly. Face to face. And be true to what you want. If you break up with them, don't just take them back because you feel bad. That won't do anyone any favours. It will just prolong the pain. If you think you want to be with someone else, other than the person you are with, then you owe it to them to be honest. Cheating is a horrible thing, no matter if you're doing it or it is being done to you. It is selfish and hurtful and nobody ever wins.

— *"I broke up with my boyfriend on Facebook. I sent him a picture of me kissing another guy. When I think about it now I feel really mean. If someone did that to me... OMG... that would suck."* — *Jane, 17*

— *"I reckon the worst feeling in the word is being dumped."* — *Mary, 16*

— *"He cheated on me and I set fire to his favourite shoes. His mum told my mum and they made me buy him new ones."* — *Kimberly, 17*

— *"I just wanted to throw eggs and bricks and flames at his house. I didn't. But fuck I wanted to."* — *Samantha, 17*

— *"Chocolate and ice cream and Bridget Jones. That's what I did"* — *Geraldine, 17*

Porn and Erotica!

What is porn?

Porn is the visual representation of sex. So basically pictures and movies of people having sex or participating in various sexual acts. eg. X-Rated moves, Penthouse and Playboy magazines, sexual internet pictures and movies.

What is erotica?

Erotica is the written version of porn. So things like *Fifty Shades of Grey* or sexy internet fan fiction, or Penthouse Forum letters.

However, in saying that, there are many different categories of both and some erotica can be classed as porn and vice versa. Some can be pretty tame (like a picture of boobs) and some can be completely wild and often confusing to young people, and even old people, seriously! Some of the stuff I've seen during my time of researching and writing about sex has made the hairs on the back of my neck stand up, and I'm a grown adult with over twenty years of experience in sex research, so I absolutely understand that, with all the taboo around sex and the fact that so many people don't like talking about it, it can be tricky to work out what's what, and what's 'normal'

When I was younger, in the old prehistoric days before the internet, porn wasn't too easy to come by unless you accidentally stumbled across your dad's playboy mags or video collection. Really the closest thing most of us got to porn was watching tacky 80s movies like Revenge of the Nerds that always had bare boobs in them. There was a "sex"show on TV for a while, but it was a little bit tacky, and most of us weren't allowed to watch it anyway, I do have very fond memories of the steamy soap operas they played in the afternoons with soft Vaseline-lensed sex scenes and loads of neck kissing, and bed sheets that strangely always went up to her boobs but seemed to stop at the guys' waists. They could be way sexy and fun to watch.

Every now and then, someone at school would come across what we called bush porn. And no, I'm not referring to 70s and 80s 'pre-Brazilian' bush, I mean old Playboys or movies someone had hidden or stashed away in a park or in the bush. It would be passed around the school or the group til someone's mum found it and threw it away. But it was always (especially compared to these days) super tame stuff that rarely showed anything major like (gasp) actual sex or, if it did, anything other than your standard in-out-blowjob-orgasm stuff.

These days, if you're not careful, you can put something completely innocent into a search engine and be horrified at some of the things that come up. A few years ago a friend wanted to start up a little cafe and Googled a word, a very innocent word, and was completely blown away at the explicit pictures and content that flooded her screen. It's everywhere and, like I said, some of it is just ... *scary*.

One thing you must always remember with porn is, like with pictures of models in magazines, or burgers on the McDonalds menu, it's all a bit fake. Put on for show. Not only is it done in specific ways to highlight and enhance certain things, it's also not at all a true representation of what sex is and what is expected of you. The faces, the positions, the noises the, *everything*. It is all done for entertainment sake and is not a how-to guide.

Sex is about feeling good, so if it doesn't feel good, or makes you uncomfortable then it's just not worth doing. You should never feel pressured into "performing" like a porn star, or doing the things they do in movies and pictures.

Sure, its fun to experiment and try new things, but you should never feel obligated to do it just because someone else wants you to.

For example, something that almost always happens in pornography is anal sex. After talking to a bunch of girls in the past few years I have discovered that many of them are doing this act not because they WANT to, but because they feel EXPECTED to. Nope. Wrong. Uh-uh. Anal sex, like anything else sexual, is a matter of personal choice and many, many girls do not enjoy it or have any inclination to try. A lot of guys will tell you how good it feels and that you should give it a try, but here is the kicker; a lot of guys think *that* because, for them, it actually CAN feel great. Even more than it can for girls. Don't get me wrong, there are many females who enjoy it too, but the reason males think it feels good is because their G-spot is actually located in their anus and it can create really enjoyable sensations for them.

This does not make them gay (not that there's anything wrong with that). This does not mean anything at all. It's just the physical way our bodies are built. The male G-spot (like the female one) is associated with the prostate gland (remember when we were talking about squirting?) and in males that just happens to be inside their bum.

Another thing pornography shows a lot of is females being covered in cum (semen). Whether on their faces or their bodies or into their mouths. Again, this is not something you have to do. Firstly, as we have talked about previously, it can be dangerous to your health having unprotected contact with bodily fluids and secondly, if it makes you feel gross, or disgusted or degraded in any way, then it is not for you. Again, like anal sex, these things are all up to the individual involved, and some people really enjoy the feeling and taste and all that stuff. But if you don't, then there is no reason to do it.

So that's looking at pretty much your standard porn formula that you come across, which is most often: Sex, change position, sex, anal sex, blow job, cum... But what about when you come across something a bit more full on, something that might be considered taboo? Something that looks completely insane, or painful or weird or gross? What if it kind of scares you? Or freaks you out? Or, on the other side of the same coin, what happens if something you discover is a bit different from the standard and it appeals to you and turns you on? You think maybe it's something you might want to try? Well, you know what? That's okay too. Being curious and turned on and interested is perfectly normal and does not make you some sort of perverted freak.

Being confronted with something that makes you feel a bit uncomfortable (or downright off-putting or offensive) can be hard. It can make you feel all sorts of things and can make you question everything you thought about sex and pleasure and "why the hell is she doing that it's so horrid I can't bear to even look!" That's okay. It happens. It's happened to me. The best thing to do when that does happens is to switch it off, take a deep breath and go do something else. If it is really disturbing, to the point of distress, it is really important to talk to someone about it. Someone who can help you to understand what it is you've just seen and maybe help you figure it all out a bit better.

My friends and I watch porn all the time. It's so funny. The faces! OMG they are hilarious. - Kimberly 17

I really like gay porn. Like boys with boys. Is that weird cos I'm a girl? I don't know... But it's hot. - Kathy 16

— My girlfriend and I saw a porn clip that made us nearly vomit. Serious gross stuff with poo and wee and stuff. Do people actually do that? It's just... Uurrggg. — Jess, 15

— I go online and read lesbian erotica all the time. I like the fan fiction stuff that has TV and book characters I like in it. Hermione and Luna ones are good. — Deb, 17

— My mum has like a million Mills and Boon books. I sneak them into my room and read the sex bits over and over and play with myself... And then sometimes I think that maybe my mum has done the same and I feel a bit weird. I should buy my own books. — Bec, 16

— I saw some pictures online with this guy all tied up and a girl giving him a blowjob. It was so sexy it made me want to do it. I still do. I just don't know how to ask my boyfriend if he'll let me tie him up. — Samantha, 17

— So embarrassing. My mum found a bunch of porn pictures I had on my phone. She made me delete it all and grounded me for a week. Now I have to remember to delete it after I've looked at it. — Karen, 15

The pros and pitfalls of taking and sending nudes!

Before I start this section I want to note that it was really hard to write. This is for a few reasons. The main one being that it absolutely sucks that I even have to write it but I do. I do because the world is full of douche bags and idiots and there's such a huge lack of respect and maturity when it comes to sex and sexuality. And this is the world over I mean, not just for teenagers. But the other reason it was hard was because the act of sexting and taking naked pics and stuff like that is something that should be fun and awesome and enjoyable and private. I don't want to have to tell you all the crap and warnings that I have to. I don't want you to feel that anything some dickhead person does with your words or photographs later on to humiliate and upset you is your fault. Because it isn't at all. It's perfectly normal to want to do all those things, and (with exceptions to the laws stated below) perfectly within all your rights to do them. But unfortunately, because of this lack of respect for women, for boundaries and for consent, I have to write it, and warn you, and make you aware that bad shit can happen and it can make your life hell.

Yes, like I said, sending sexy text messages and emails and stuff can be really fun and exciting, I know. It can get you more turned on than reading erotica and watching porn and it can be great material for masturbating over. The only problem is, and it's a huge one, is once you have sent it, once you have said all the things you have said, it is out of your hands and on the screen of someone else who, for whatever reason, may not be as trustworthy or as secretive as you want and need them to be. The thing about the internet and technology is once it is out there, once it has been posted, it is there **forever**. It can come back at any time and bite you on the arse. It can get forwarded to everyone you know, including your family members. It can be printed out a billion times and posted up on the walls of the school toilets. It can be laughed at and ridiculed and make you feel like things

> *Remember the age of consent per state in Australia is as follows:*
>
> *NSW, VIC, ACT, QLD, NT, WA – 16*
>
> *SA, TAS - 17*

will never ever calm down and go back to the way they were. It's a horrible feeling. Like a big, fat stab in the gut. Especially after the original things you have written were probably rather enjoyable at the time.

When it comes to sending photographs of yourself this kind of thing can be even worse. Not only could the entire school or even town see pictures you thought were private, but also, if you are under the age of consent it is also illegal. Like really, really illegal! If you are under the age of consent and you send a photograph of your boobs or other bits to someone else it is actually considered to be producing, possessing and distributing child pornography and these sort of breaches of the law can come with very severe and sometimes life altering consequences.

As with texts and emails and all things written electronically once it has been sent you have absolutely NO control over where it goes. *None*. If you are caught and found guilty both you and the person you sent it to can face hefty fines and punishments and you may even be put on the Sex Offender Registry for around eight years. Eight years!! And every prospective employer (especially if you want to work in the public sector or with children or aged people, or a government department or anywhere really) will be able to see this. So just think, if you are 15, and you send a picture of your boobs to your 15 year old boyfriend and it is caught by someone who decides to take it to the law, when you are 22 years old and you go for that job interview and your future employer decides to do a background check on you... Let me tell you, you probably won't get that job for being a registered sex offender. It really is that harsh.

And now with those disgusting "revenge porn" sites popping up all over the place, who knows where your private and personal pictures may end up or who will see them.

I'm really not trying to scare you at all. It absolutely sucks that something as fun and exciting as showing off and being sexy to someone you feel close to has the ability to turn into something so sour and embarrassing. It's a horrible breach of your privacy and trust. There are absolutely no acceptable reasons for it to be done. It's just plain disrespectful.

Wanting to take a sexy selfie is, as I said, your right to do so if you want, but please be aware of all the consequences. It is perfectly okay to say no. You are not a prude, a cock tease, a bitch or anything if you say no. Just as you are not a slut or a whore or anything if you decide to do it. You're just a person making a choice. If you do say no, and they continue to ask and hassle you, then it is sexual harassment and can even be prosecuted as such. You should never feel pressured to do anything you don't want to do.

— *"My boyfriend and I sent each other naked pictures of ourselves. When we broke up he sent them to his friends. The school found out and we both got in heaps of trouble. My mum wanted to call the police. I'm really glad she didn't."* — *Josie, 16*

— *"The guys at school take pics of their dicks and post them on Facebook. It's gross."* — *Leigh, 17*

— *"My dad found a picture on my phone of my boobs. He took my phone off me and told me I could go to jail. I don't know if that's true but it scared me enough not to do it again."* — *Lucy, 16*

— *"I know a few girls who sent movies of themselves fingering themselves to boys. Stupid idiots didn't realise the whole school saw them."* — *Geraldine, 17*

— *"There's no way I would do that ever. I'm not stupid"* — *Bec, 16*

— *"I take pics all the time. It makes me feel sexy. I know it's a bit dangerous, but I still do it."* — *Kimberly, 17*

Every second of every day over 30 million people are watching porn on their computers. So don't think you're some sort of weirdo, perverted freak. We are all doing it!

According to a study done by the Kinsey Institute at the University of Indiana when watching porn, most men look at faces. Yep. Not boobs. Not bums. Not vag. Faces. In North Korea, watching porn can get you the death penalty.

The University of Montreal tried to write a conclusive study on the differences between men who watch and men who don't watch porn. But they were unable to finish the study because they could not find a single guy who did not watch it.

Toys
and
Other Fun Things!

Using your fingers to play and reach orgasm is great fun, but imagine this. What if you could increase those feelings by like a hundred? A good sex toy can do exactly that!

Sex toys usually come in two sorts, dildos and vibrators. A dildo is like a fake penis (although it doesn't necessarily look like one) with no motor, where as a vibrator is the same thing with a power source that makes it buzz and spin and whir and pulse. Some require batteries to use, others come with rechargeable power sources built in, and others you plug directly into the wall socket and use from there. Some toys are water resistant, meaning you can take them into the shower, and some are completely waterproof which means you can use them in the bath. They can come in all sizes and strengths and shapes too. Some look like regular dicks, all veins and balls and stuff, some just look like smooth coloured columns, others can be shaped like little animals and then some are like mixtures of them all. One of the most popular vibrators (mostly because it was featured in the TV show *Sex And The City*) is known as the rabbit vibe. This is a phallic (penis shaped) toy with an attachment on the side usually shaped like a rabbit. The main part, usually containing pearly beads which spin and vibrate is inserted into the vagina to stimulate the vaginal wall and G-spot, and the rabbit bit quite often actually shaped like a little sitting rabbit with two rubbery ears, vibrates with a little buzzing bullet all of its own and stimulates the clitoris.

Like the little rabbit attachment, bullet vibes (so called because they are usually shaped and sized like a bullet) are also a very popular toy, especially for people just starting out on their sex toy experimentation. These are usually only about the size of a lipstick 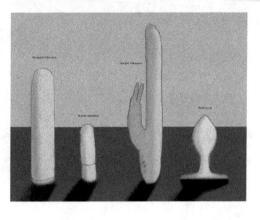 (although some are smaller and some slightly larger) which can pack a real punch with their powerful buzzes. In fact, you can actually buy these in the shape of a lipstick tube so you can stash it away in your bag or something and no one will know what it is if they happen to come across it.

When wanting to play with sex toys anally you must only use toys that have been designed for anal use. These will ALWAYS have a flattened or ringed base that is wider than the widest bit of the toy. This is for the very important act of making sure it does not get lost inside you. In your vagina, you have a cervix that will stop anything for becoming irretrievably lost inside your body. Your bum does not have this. Basically, with lots of twists and turns, the butt hole is a tunnel that leads to your mouth. So if something gets stuck inside, it can really, really get stuck. And that is not a trip to the hospital you want to have to take!

Buying Toys

If you're under 18 it can be a bit tricky to source sex toys. There are no specific laws that state the age in which you can buy them, but every Australian state except Queensland (which has no proper regulations or laws on adult material.) has laws that require you to be 18 years old to enter an adult shop. Although in saying that a lot of stores do self regulate and will not let a minor inside. If you have a credit or debit card you can buy them online and some companies still accept money orders which you can get from a post office, but it can be hard to know what to buy, what sort, how much to spend and what the best one is for you. It is really useful to research the toys before you buy them because, obviously, there is no try-before-you-buy when it comes to these items. You can research them by looking online at reviews and a lot of magazines often do sealed section toy reviews where you can get heaps of information about the toys, their functions and what they can feel like. If you have a friend or older sister or even a mum you can talk to about these things, that's also a really good way to find out about them. Also, an older sister or mum can buy them for you in a sex shop if you trust them enough to ask.

Alternatives to Sex Toys

Because it can be hard to get sex toys when you're under 18 a lot of teenagers I know use other items and implements to get the same sensation. If you decide to use something other than a specific toy I will suggest you ALWAYS use a condom with these things because they are not meant to be used as toys, but they can really imitate the sensations and work just as well. After speaking to all the young women I have over the years, I've learnt that probably the most common outside implement girls use to masturbate with is the tap, shower head or bath faucet. It's free, easy, and in a place where you can usually be guaranteed of privacy and no-one walking in on you. Running water against your genitals can be really good and, as long as you don't push it directly up into your vagina, it's safe and pretty easy not to make too much of a mess (except splashing water) as you're already in the bath or shower.

Food such as cucumbers and zucchinis are also used a lot as an alternative to a dildo, but you must be really careful not to get any food inside your vagina. This can really screw up the bacteria and PH levels in there and lead to things like thrush. I probably wouldn't recommend it as such, but I know girls use them, so I need to let you know it can be unsafe. An alternative to food, and a lot safer to use internally, are things like the handle of a hairbrush, a thin deodorant spray or other things like that. Make sure they are smooth with no seams or jagged edges that could cut or scratch you. Be slow and careful and, again, ALWAYS COVER WITH A CONDOM.

For vibrating alternatives I know a few girls who first started out with electric toothbrushes. I've used one in my mouth as a toothbrush and have been all, "Wow, I bet this would feel good somewhere else!" So I totally get it. It's also something you can walk into any supermarket and buy and no-one will even look at you twice. As with the other things, always use a condom, and make sure you use the flat end, not the bristles because *ouch*!

Then there are toys for kids that shake and whir. I read a news story a couple of years ago about the increase of sales among teenage girls of a vibrating Harry Potter flying broom toy which, when sat on in the hobby horse style gave similar sensations to that of a vibrator.

— *"My electric toothbrush is fucking awesome. Best invention ever. I don't think I've ever actually brushed my teeth with it"* — Kimberly, 17

— *"I use running water from our shower-head. It's one of those ones you can take off the wall. It feels really really good."* — Susan, 14

— *"Before I bought my first dildo I used cumbers and zucchinis. They are better when they aren't freezing cold, straight from the fridge. I tried a carrot once too, but it was all pointy and a bit weird feeling"* — Cate, 18

Playing with Toys

Depending on the toy you buy, there are a number of different techniques to use to get the best out of them. The most common way to play (but by no means necessarily the best for you) is to hold the buzzing end of the toy against your clitoris. A lot of toys come with different speed settings and pulse and vibration settings, so it can be a matter of pressing through all the features to see which one works the best for you. The next way they are used is to put them inside your vagina and use them to stimulate the G-spot (located on the front wall about half way up). A lot of toys these days come with special curls and knobs in them specifically to hit that little spot, but, as with everything and everyone it's different for different people so sometimes a bit of wiggling around and experimentation is the way to go. Probably the best way to know if you've hit your G-spot or not is a sort of odd sensation like you need to wee. This can freak some people out and make them stop because they are afraid of wetting themselves, and that's completely understandable, but it's actually not a bladder thing at all. Pushing through this sensation can often lead to intense orgasms and even female ejaculation, usually called squirting.

Tips For Using Toys

Battery Operated Toys: Try and buy toys that require normal type batteries like AA and AAA. Sometimes they use weird ones like watch batteries or big C ones and they aren't cheap and not always easy to find. Always use cheap batteries. An expensive one, like a lithium battery or high powered one, can ruin the motor too quickly.

Rechargeable Toys: Mostly these need to be charged before you use them and will take anything from two hours to around 24 to be fully charged. They have usually got a little light which will indicate when they are ready to use. Some of them can last weeks before you have to recharge, and others will use their power quicker. Always read the little information brochure which comes with it to find out what's what.

Testing Toys: Although you can't actually test them out properly in the shops (and not at all if you buy online) if you do get a chance to feel the buzz before you get it, the best place to feel how strong it is, is on the end of your nose. It sounds weird, but the tip of your nose is very sensitive and just holding it lightly against it will give you an indication of how strong the vibrations will be.

Using Lube: Lube (short for lubrication) is a gel like substance used for helping make things a bit more slippery. Trust me when I tell you there's nothing very sexy about trying to play with a toy (or have sex) when you aren't wet enough and, even if you are, a little extra help never goes astray. Lubes are mostly either water based or silicone based and it is really important to know what you are buying depending on the material your toy is made of. If it is made of silicone (and most of them are these days) do not, I repeat DO NOT, use a silicone based lubricant. This is because when the two silicone products come into contact the silicone gel eats away at the silicone covering on the toy and kind of melts it and wrecks it. Silicone lubes can also leave stain marks on bed sheets etc, whereas water-based lubes are non staining, non sticky, and perfect to use with all toys. There are all sorts of fancy shmancy lubes out there, but really, all you need is a basic water-based supermarket brand. Something like "Wet Stuff" or "Four Seasons" is perfectly fine for getting things fun and slippery. They can be bought at any supermarket or chemist and they're usually under $10.

Cleaning and Storing Toys

Always clean your toys after you use them. You can buy specific toy cleaners at sex shops, but really all you need is a baby wet-wipe or something similar. I say baby wipes rather than soap and water, because soap can often be high in pH levels and can affect the bacteria levels in your body and make you susceptible to things like thrush. Make sure you read the instructions carefully so you don't end up water-damaging a toy's battery source.

It's a good idea to remove the batteries from a toy when you're not using it. Batteries can get old and leak and damage a toy and it also stops them accidentally getting switched on and running out of charge before you get to use it again, or (even worse) it could turn on when you don't want it to. I once had the embarrassing moment of going through airport security, with my bag being opened by the guard at the end, and as she rummaged around must have accidentally knocked the button and not only scared the pants off her when it happened, but it also embarrassed us both! If the toy you're using is rechargeable and doesn't have batteries, then quite often they have a "lock" feature which means you can't accidentally push a button and it start going off. Excellent feature for travelling!

If you have more than one toy and they are made of TPR Gel (the see-through jelly type stuff), do not store them together. As with the silicone lube reacting and damaging the toy, this will happen when two jelly toys come into contact. Also TPR Gel is a porous material, which means it can trap bacteria and all sorts of things in the material, no matter how much you clean it, and that can be super dangerous for your body, Some toys come with handy little pouches to store them in, or you could just use a sock, or a pair of stockings.

All in all, sex toys are a great little enhancement to masturbation. They can give you sensations you've not experienced and open up the world of orgasmic excitement even more. I've heard old wives tales tell of using a toy too much being able to damage the nerve endings in your clitoris and make sensations less, but this is not true. It can mean you get a bit more used to the bigger buzzes than just fingers, but there is no lasting damage you can do. If you do find you're getting a bit used to it, you can always stop for a little while and then return to using it after you've had a bit of a break.

Sharing Toys.

To be honest it's not a super great idea to share toys because a lot of STIs can be transmitted through vaginal fluids but, if you are going to, the best advice I can give you is to use a condom with it, and to make sure you swap the condom between people. Again, always clean your toys after use and make sure they're properly switched off and batteries removed afterwards. If you happen to be using a toy for both vaginal and anal play then you need to make sure it's a specific anal toy, and definitely use condoms and swap them between uses. The bacteria from your anus can really, really, REALLY screw up your vagina. Never let anyone or anything go straight from anal to vaginal play without changing the condom, or washing your hands. Ever!

Body Care

Contraception, condoms and caring for yourself.

The next step in being ready to have sex for the first time is making sure you have the right equipment. Don't panic! I'm not talking about handcuffs and whips and chocolate body paint, there's plenty of time for those things. I'm talking about the two essential items no sexual person should ever leave the house without. I am talking about condoms and lubricant (lube).

Condoms are your number one safe sex item. When used properly they are 99.9% effective against pregnancy and most sexually transmitted infections (STIs). I say most, because there are a few STIs that condoms can't protect you from, namely herpes and pubic lice – but there are other ways to prevent them and I will go into that later. Please be aware that the contraceptive pill, although great as contraception will not protect you from getting sick. At all! Even if you take the pill it is absolutely imperative you also use condoms. Every time you have sex.

Don't be embarrassed to buy condoms. You can get them everywhere from your local supermarket to a petrol station to a specialist sex shop. They are also often available for free at sexual health clinics and Family Planning centres. You don't have to be eighteen to buy them and you don't need to over think it. Forget about colours and flavours and ribbed-for-her-pleasures, you just need a basic latex condom and you can get a pack of six from around $5.00. Be aware that some people can get a reaction to latex, so for them there are also latex free brands. They may be a little more pricey, but not by much.

Lube is there to help things slide a little bit easier and make the experience less uncomfortable and painful than it could otherwise be without. Yes, when you're aroused your body produces its own lubricant, however a little help is always good and when you're nervous, like you most likely will be on your first time, your vagina has a tendency to clench up and dry out and that is no fun for anyone. There is a great meme/ quote that talks about the importance of lube by comparing it to going down a water slide when there is no water. This is a very accurate description. Seriously, ouch!

Again, don't worry about all the extra fancy things when you're first experimenting with sex. Arousal gels and flavoured lubes are all very well and good, but they are not the be all and end all of sex and if you have too many things to think about and decide on it will only add to your nervousness. Just get a basic water-based lubricant like Wet Stuff, available for super cheap at the supermarket or chemist, and that will do the trick. I cannot stress enough that you must buy a water-based one. Oil-based lubricants like Vaseline, baby oil or even coconut oil will react against the latex in the condom and degrade it and even fully break it, and that is something you want to prevent happening at all costs.

How to put on a condom

Putting on a condom can be a bit fiddly at first, but once you have the knack it's fairly easy. They come all rolled up and flat in a packet and they only roll one way. It's good to practice on a cucumber or banana or a sex toy first, just to get the hang of it. Hold it lightly around the rolled up ring and gently squeeze the tip of it. This it to make sure no air gets inside as you roll it down. Hold it on

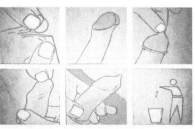

Top Left: Check Expiry on package. Open condom.
Top Middle: Make sure the penis is erect.
Top Right: Place condom on tip of penis, and squeeze the air out of the tip of the condom between thumb and index finger.

Bottom Left: Carefully roll condom down penis with one hand, while squeezing air out of tip with the other.
Bottom Middle: You are now ready for sexual activity.
Bottom Right: When you are finished using your condom, wrap it in tissue and throw it in the bin. DO NOT flush down the toilet.

the top of the penis/cucumber/toy and gently roll it down while still squeezing the tip. Make sure it rolls down to the bottom of the penis.

It is almost impossible, and pretty useless, to put a condom on a soft penis, so you must wait for it to be fully erect. You can have lots of fun doing this! The whole process of becoming aroused, for both male and females, should be as fun as the actual act of having sex. Use the time to explore and learn about each other's bodies. When it comes down to it, penetration is such a minor part of the whole sex thing. The kissing and touching and playing and exploring is just as important and actually makes the act of sexual intercourse far more fun.

So what happens if the condom breaks or comes off or you have unprotected sex?

Every now and then a condom will fail to work. This can be for a few different reasons. If there is not enough lubricant, either natural vaginal wetness or the stuff you buy, sometimes the dryness can pull at the condom and result in it tearing. Like I said before, oil based lubricants (like Vaseline, coconut oil, or baby oil) will eat at the latex and cause it to tear, so never, ever use them. Sometimes a condom can slip off the penis during sex. If this happens it can often be a little bit of a fiddle inside yourself to retrieve it, but it is important to get it out. Do not use tongs or any other kind of implement to try and reach it. You can really damage yourself that way. If it proves impossible to get out it you will need to go see a doctor and they will find it for you.

In the event of a condom failing the first thing you should do is get to a chemist and get the morning after pill. Seriously. You do not need to go to a doctor, you do not need a prescription, and you have around 72 hours, or four days to get it (although it is recommended you take it as close to 24 hours after for the best results). It will cost around $20 - $30 but that can be less if you have a Health Care card. The pharmacist will need to ask you a few questions, but it is completely anonymous and you do not have to give any personal identifying information.

Very rarely the pharmacist may have to refer you to a doctor. You must tell the pharmacist if you have high blood pressure, diabetes, liver disease, had a stroke or breast cancer and if you are taking any other medications. All these things can alter its effectiveness or cause you to become unwell.

What is the morning after pill?

Basically the MAP can stop a pregnancy before it starts by stopping, or delaying, the release of eggs from your ovaries. It doesn't stop fertilisation, it is NOT an abortion pill and most importantly it will not prevent you from getting any Sexually Transmitted Infections (STIs) or work as an ongoing contraceptive. If taken in the first 24 hours, is 95% effective in making sure you have not conceived. After 72 hours this percentage falls to 85% and anything after that the effectiveness drops significantly.

Side Effects?

The side effects can include feeling a bit sick, vomiting and tiredness. You may also get tummy pain and diarrhoea, headache or dizziness and sore boobs. You may also bleed like you're getting a period. If you do vomit within a couple of hours of taking it, you will need to get another pill. Pharmacists will often provide an anti-nausea tablet with the pill to try and prevent this from happening.

If the pill is effective, you should get your period around the normal time, but be aware it could also be a little early or late.

What else should I do?

Not only can unprotected sex lead to pregnancy, it can also make you very sick with STIs. If you have had unprotected sex or the condom has failed, like its broken or slipped off, you need to go and get yourself tested. Unfortunately some STIs do not show up immediately on tests and so you may also need to get a follow up test. Please have a good read of the STI section in this book. It lists the STIs you can get, how they affect you and how you can treat and prevent them. There is also a list of clinics and places you can go to be tested both in that section and at the back of the book. It is highly important to keep you and your sexual partners safe and disease free, as well as consent THIS is one of the most important things when it comes to being sexually active.

What happens if I DO become pregnant?

If your contraception fails and you become pregnant you basically have three options. You can terminate the pregnancy via a surgical abortion or by taking the abortion pill, RU486. You can have the baby and give it up for adoption, or you can have the baby and raise it.

What is The Pill?

The pill is a daily tablet that contains synthetic oestrogen and progesterone (naturally occurring hormones in women) and works by stopping your ovaries from releasing eggs. It can also create a thicker lining to your cervix which can stop sperm from entering.

If correctly used it can be 99.7% effective in stopping pregnancy.

It must be taken EVERY DAY for it to be effective. If you miss just one it can screw it all up and cease to work.

The seven little red pills you get in the packet are just sugar pills. They stop the birth control hormone and allow you to have a period. If you miss one of these it will not stop the effectiveness of the pill, but they are really useful for the remembering the routine of taking one every day.

The pill WILL NOT stop you from getting an STI.

You need a prescription from your doctor to get it and if you are on certain medications it can alter its effect.

The pill can help in reducing severe period pains and mood swings connected with menstruation, and has been known to be effective in helping clear up (or at least reduce) pimples.

If you have a really heavy flow, or your period is irregular the pill can help to make it a bit more manageable. However, it can also be a factor in deep vein thrombosis (blood clots), heart attacks and strokes.

These are all very personal decisions and should not be taken lightly. Please be aware that laws regarding abortion are different state to state, and are constantly being changed or reviewed so it really is imperative to look up the regulations and laws for where you live, and also get into contact with family planning and non-religious, independent abortion support organisations that can help you with your choice and ability to do so. Although ultimately the choice of what to do in this situation is up to you, it is absolutely important you talk to someone about it. If you really cannot talk to your mother, father, guardian or a close older female relative or friend (even a school teacher you trust) then the next best thing (and something you should do even if you *can* talk to a relative or close adult friend) is contact a family planning counsellor. They are professionally trained to help guide you through your choices and will be absolutely objective and neutral in your decision making. There is a list at the end of this chapter of clinics and counselling services available.

Remember it is YOUR body and YOUR choice.

Other Forms of Birth Control and Safe Sex items

Implanon

This is a small rod, about the size of a matchstick, which is inserted into the skin of your arm by a doctor. It releases a hormone called progestogen and works in a similar way to the pill in stopping the release of eggs. It can be 99.9% effective. It lasts for around three years. In some cases it can stop periods altogether, in others it can result in slightly irregular bleeding, and in others it can have absolutely no side effects at all. It can sometimes cause weight gain, sore breasts, headaches and skin changes. It will NOT protect you from STIs

Depo Provera

Depo Provera is an injection (in the bum cheek) given to you by a doctor every 12 weeks (three months). Like the pill and the Implanon, it contains hormones similar to ones your body naturally produces and stops your ovaries from releasing eggs. It can be from around 94-99% effective in stopping you from getting pregnant. It can result in changes to your period, usually in lighter bleeding or having none at all. It can cause weight gain, mood swings and pimples. It will NOT stop you from getting an STI.

Female Condom

The female condom is very similar to a male one, except instead of going over the penis it is inserted into the vagina. It has a soft ring on both sides and the larger end covers some of the vulva (outer lips). When used properly it can be up to 95% effective. Because it covers the outer areas it can be help reduce the spread of STIs like herpes and warts, but only if infected areas are covered. It can sometimes slip off when the penis withdraws, or the penis can accidentally slide in between the condom and the vagina when inserting, so you need to be careful.

Dental Dams

Dental Dams are not a contraceptive in any way. They are used for oral sex (vaginal or anal) on females and can reduce the risk of STIs. Basically they are a thin square piece of latex that you hold over the vulva or anus while you lick it. They can be really tricky to use, but are definitely a good idea for protecting against things like herpes and genital warts. Do NOT use something like Gladwrap as an alternative. But a condom split down the side and opened flat can work too.

The Ugly Side Of Sex

STIs

VD, STDs, The Clap, Cupid's Itch, Dick Cheese, Fanny Scratch, The Dose.

STI stands for Sexually Transmitted Infections and are most often spread by bodily fluids coming into contact with one another. They can be really nasty and totally fuck up your life. And I mean really. Some can lead to infertility and even death. The best way to avoid getting one is to never have sex, but really, that's completely unrealistic in the context of this book, so let's move on to how you can do your best to avoid them and protect yourself and others from catching something horrible.

Your best defence against most STIs is using condoms. I say most because there are some that condoms can't protect you from and we will get to that soon, but first let's talk about some of the most common STIs.

Chlamydia

What is it?

Chlamydia is the most common STI in young people in Australia today. In fact, since the year 2000 the number of reported cases have quadrupled and of those cases 80% of them have been in people aged 15 to 29. It can affect both males and females and is caused by a bacteria. Chlamydia can be contracted through all types of sex (vaginal, anal and oral) and if left untreated can cause serious pelvic inflammation and fertility issues in women and long-term infection and pain and discomfort in the testicles for men. It can also infect the anus and the mouth/throat too.

Symptoms

The main problem with Chlamydia (I mean apart from the fact you have Chlamydia) is there are very few symptoms until it gets to the dangerously damaging side. Girls may get spot bleeding between periods or after sex and pelvic and urination pain, and guys may get a clear discharge from their penises or pain when they urinate, but really, it's mostly undetectable without a test. If you have had unprotected sex then I highly suggest you go and get tested.

Diagnosis and Treatment

It's a painless although sometimes slightly uncomfortable swab test (which means they take a sample of discharge from inside your vagina) but, for your own safety and peace of mind as well as others', it's worth it.

Chlamydia is treated by antibiotics. Sometimes just a single dose will get rid of it, but other times you may need to go on a seven day course. It's important to inform anyone you have had sex with that you have tested positive so they can go and get tested too.

Gonorrhoea

What is it?

Gonorrhoea is the second most reported STI in Australia and, like Chlamydia, if left untreated can lead to serious pelvic inflammatory disease and infertility issues in both males and females. It is spread by unprotected sex (vaginal, anal and oral)

Symptoms

As with Chlamydia, gonorrhoea has very few symptoms until it's too late. There may be smelly discharge or pain when going to the toilet but really, it's hard to tell if you have it without a test.

Diagnosis and Treatment

Gonorrhoea can be detected with a basic urine or swab test and is treated with antibiotics. Again, it is important to tell previous sexual partners that you have been diagnosed so they can go and get tested too.

Syphilis

What is it?

Syphilis is an STI which has been around for centuries. I remember in history class learning that Henry the Eighth died of it, and I always thought it was one of those things like smallpox that had been basically eradicated. I was wrong. It hasn't and recently, much to my surprise and sadness, it has made quite a comeback. It's a bacterial infection and can be really, really bad.

Symptoms

At first syphilis is pretty undetectable without tests. Although in some cases you can get a sort of painless ulcer which can, in turn, spread like a rash all over your body. You may also get swollen glands and feel a bit like you have the flu.

If you do not get treatment for it things can get really bad. You can suffer from heart failure and terrible pains that shoot through your body and painful oozing ulcers all over and it can also send you crazy. As in actually mentally crazy.

Diagnosis and Treatment

Syphilis is tested by a swab taken from an infected sore and is treated with penicillin.

Herpes

What is it?

Herpes is one of the most common STIs in Australia these days and is a strain of virus similar to that of the cold sores you get on your mouth. In fact around one in ten people carry the virus. It is spread through vaginal, anal and oral sex and from genital skin to skin contact. If herpes is present on an area not covered by a condom, then you are at risk of contracting it even if you use a condom. Even though mouth cold sores are a slightly different sample of the virus, if transferred to the genitals it will mutate into genital herpes.

Symptoms

Sometimes there are no signs at all that you are carrying the virus, but most commonly there are blisters and sores on and around the genitals. You can get headaches and fevers and swollen glands and have pain when going to the toilet. The first outbreak is usually the worst.

Diagnosis and Treatment

There is NO CURE for herpes. There are medications that can help manage outbreaks but, once you have it you will always have it. If left untreated it can manifest into meningitis (A disease of the brain membranes and spinal cord which can cause death). If you discover blisters, or someone you have had sex with has the disease you must get tested. Testing is just a simple swab taken from a sore.

HIV/AIDS

What is it?

HIV (Human Immunodeficiency Virus) is the virus that causes AIDS (Acquired Immunodeficiency Syndrome). It is spread by blood to blood contact and unprotected sex. It can be transferred by vaginal and anal sex, and even by mother to baby while breastfeeding, and by sharing needles. It is very rare (although not unheard of) for HIV to be contracted by oral sex. It is often falsely referred to as a disease only gay men get. This is absolutely not true. In fact, in 2009 over a quarter of all positive diagnoses were by unprotected heterosexual sex. If it is left untreated, HIV turns into AIDS and (by 2010) was the cause of nearly 7000 deaths in Australia.

You cannot get HIV/AIDS by sharing drinks or food, touching someone, toilet seats or mosquitoes.

> In the talk of HIV and AIDS in the media, you may have heard about the medication, PrEP. PrEP stands for Pre-exposure Prophylaxis. It is a relatively new, preventative medication that contains two different medicines: Tenofovir and Emtricitabine. This is a drug that is useful for people who are in high risk categories for HIV and, if taken every day, can help to prevent the virus from becoming a permanent infection if it comes into contact with your bodily fluids. It is NOT a cure and should not be used in place of other preventative methods like using condoms.

Symptoms

Unfortunately HIV has very few symptoms and some people can carry the disease for years without knowing they have it. Sometimes there are flu-like symptoms and fatigue and weight loss, and there may also be the onset of mouth ulcers, but really it is very hard to tell until it becomes full blown AIDS and by then it is often too late.

Diagnosis and Treatment

A simple blood test is all it takes to diagnose this disease. However, because it can take a while to show up in tests, you may be required to repeat the test in three months time. Although treatments and new breakthroughs in medication are advancing all the time, there is, as yet, no cure. So once you have it, you have it for life. Antiretroviral (ART) are the main treatment, which consist of a number of different drugs, often many different tablets, taken every day for the rest of your life. The reason for taking more than one ART at a time because, after a while, the virus begins to recognise the drugs and can then mutate itself to get around it making the medication ineffective. It isn't a cure, but it can slow down the process of HIV becoming AIDS and prolong life expectancy. One of the worst things about having HIV is it completely throws out your immune system making your body unable to fight off diseases like pneumonia and certain cancers. Quite often it is these infections, and not the HIV or AIDS virus itself, that lead to death.

If you are diagnosed as positive it is imperative you tell your previous sexual partners so they can go and get tested too.

The best way to avoid contracting this deadly virus is to always use a condom. Always.

HPV/Genital Warts

What is it?

HPV (Human papillomavirus) is the virus that causes warts. There are over a hundred different strains of the wart virus, some cause the warts you get on your fingers and toes and others cause genital warts. The different strains all do different things and affect the body differently and, unlike the herpes virus that can be transferred from your mouth to your genitals; you CANNOT get genital warts by being touched on the vagina by a hand wart. Both males and females can contract it. It is caught by skin to skin contact and unprotected sex and you can get it from someone even if you cannot see any visible warts.

If you do not get it treated, some strains of the genital wart virus can lead to cancer, the most common being cervical cancer. They can be prevented in some cases by condoms, but only if the condom is covering the affected area.

Symptoms.

Unless a wart presents itself it is very tricky to know if you have the virus or not. Warts can be raised or flat against the genital skin. You could get one, or a group of them. They often look a bit like mini cauliflowers. Quite often they are completely painless, but they can be quite itchy.

Diagnosis and Treatments

If you think you may have contracted genital warts, a doctor can examine you for the warts themselves, and a pap smear (which if you are sexually active you should be having at least every two years) can detect changes in the cells of your vagina, which can often be a sign of the HPV virus being present even if there are no lumps and bumps. Sometimes warts can clear up on their own, but the virus may not, so they can regrow and come back. There are topical ointments you can use to get rid of them and other times a doctor will freeze them off with nitrogen, which can be not only uncomfortable but rather painful as well. The HPV vaccine is definitely worth getting for the prevention of not only HPV but helping reduce the risk of cervical cancer.

Hepatitis A and B

Hepatitis A is a relatively short lived virus that affects the liver, but while you have it, it can be almost debilitating. It is caught by oral to anal contact and basically needs to run its course. Most people fully recover with little to no residual effects, but in very rare cases it can cause permanent liver damage and even death. Symptoms can include nausea, fatigue, dark urine, and jaundice (the yellowing of the skin and eyes). Once you have had the virus your body is immune to further Hepatitis A infections, and there is also a vaccine available. The vaccine is usually given to people travelling to developing countries because the infection comes from ingesting faecal matter (bits of poo) which can happen in countries where water supplies may be contaminated by sewerage etc.

Hepatitis B also affects the liver and if left untreated can cause severe liver failure and other liver diseases. It is spread by exposure to infected bodily fluids including blood, semen, vaginal fluids, and breast milk. It is treated by anti-viral medications, but it isn't a cure. More a way to manage the disease. There is also a vaccine available that may require booster throughout your lifetime, but, like Hep A, without a blood test, it is quite often very hard to know you even have it unless you get very ill.

Lice/Crabs

What is it?

Pubic lice are like nits that live in your pubic hair. They can also infest your armpit hair and chest hair in males. Basically they are little blood-sucking parasites that cause redness and itching and rashes. They are most often caught by direct skin to skin contact and cannot be prevented by condoms.

Symptoms.

Redness and itching and often little bumps or welts on the pubic hair region. You can also sometimes see them crawling around. Not nice.

Diagnosis and Treatment.

Shaving off your pubic hair can help prevent them, but as we have talked about previously, pubic hair can be necessary for many reasons. You can get topical creams and ointments similar to nit creams you use on your head.

The following ailments are infections and issues that can affect your vagina but that aren't necessarily sexually transmitted, although, some sex can affect or intensify them.

Thrush

What is it?

Thrush is an infection of a yeast like bacteria that lives in your vagina and in your anus. The bacteria is always there (in larger numbers in your anus) but sometimes it can multiply and this is where the problems lie. It can be caused by things like wiping back to front after the toilet, transferring the bacteria from your anus to your vagina, using scented soaps and some perfumes, and it is really, really common if you douche. Remember how I said douching is bad? Well this is one of the reasons. It upsets all the normal bacteria levels and can make thrush thrive.

You can also get it from wearing tight jeans and knickers made from nonbreathable fabric like nylon. Other things that can cause it are antibiotics, the contraceptive pill, diabetes and pregnancy and sometimes it just happens. It's really, really common and around 75% of all women will get it in their lifetime, probably more than once. More uncommon, but not unheard of is thrush occurring in the mouth and eyes. If a mother has thrush when she gives birth she can pass it on to the newborn and it can be really bad.

It isn't transmittable by sex but it can make sex uncomfortable and some of the creams used to treat it can actually weaken condoms and cause them to break.

Symptoms.

Thrush can make your vagina really, really itchy and sore. It can cause redness and a bit of swelling (usually caused by the constant scratching) and sometimes broken vaginal skin. You can also get a thick, sticky white discharge (that looks a bit like cottage cheese) and a burning sensation when you go to the toilet.

Diagnosis and Treatment.

A simple swab test from your doctor will get it diagnosed and there are a few different pills and creams you can get and a doctor or pharmacist will be able to help you get the best one.

BV (Bacterial Vaginosis)

What is it?

A bit like thrush, BV is an imbalance of bacteria level in the vagina. Although it isn't a sexually transmitted disease it is far more common in sexual active people than in virgins and can often occur not long after having sex and can also be brought on by the presence of some STIs. It can also be caused by douching and inserting non clean items into the vagina (always clean your sex toys and use a condom if using things like food or other items!). It cannot be caught by men, however if you have a female partner it can often be transferred.

Symptoms.

Sometimes BV has no outward symptoms at all and can come and go without you even knowing you had it, but quite often there is a runny grey, white or yellow sort of discharge and it can be accompanied by a strong "fishy" smell.

Diagnosis and Treatment.

If there are no outward symptoms of BV it's hard to know if you have it and it can quite often go away on its own. If you do have symptoms a doctor can take a swab of the discharge and diagnose it that way. It is most often treated by anti-bacterial medications either taken orally or inserted into the vagina.

Cystitis or Urinary Tract Infections (UTIs)

What is it?

A UTI is an infection of the urethra (the bit where the wee comes out) and is caused by foreign bacteria getting inside the urethra. This can be caused by wiping back to front after going to the toilet, holding in your wee when you really need to go, and having a yeast infection like thrush or STIs like Chlamydia. It can also be caused by having sex (as the urethra and vagina are very close to each other) and often mild UTIs can be referred to as "Honeymoon cystitis" because of the whole 'having-lots-of-sex-on-your–honeymoon' thing.

Symptoms.

One of the tell tale signs of having a UTI is a constant, almost painful need to go to the toilet, but not being able to get more than a small amount of wee out; also a painful burning sensation when you do go and pain and tightness around the pubic bone region. In severe cases you might also have blood in your urine. If left untreated they can sometimes turn into serious kidney infections.

Diagnosis and Treatment.

If you think you may have a UTI a doctor or pharmacist can assist you in getting the right treatment. If it's not too severe there are several over the counter medications you can get (usually in a powdered drink form you add to water). A really, really good way to prevent it, and a really simple and cheap way, is to drink lots of cranberry juice. Like a glass every day will do wonders in keeping your urinary tract clean. However, if you do go a doctor to seek medical advice, let them know you're drinking cranberry juice because sometimes that can lessen the effects of some antibiotics.

— I thought I was okay cos I was on the pill so I wouldn't get pregnant. I got Chlamydia though. It was really embarrassing having to pick up the medicine. I felt like everyone knew what I

had done. I always use condoms now. — Samantha, 17

— No one told me I would get sick; I thought the pill was enough. It wasn't. I got Chlamydia and gonorrhoea and only found out because my period was weird and I thought maybe I was pregnant. — Suze, 16

— I was with a boy and about a month later he called and told me he had herpes. It was the worst thing in the world waiting to get tested and the results. I am so glad it came up negative. I don't know what I would have done! — Geraldine, 17

— Thrush is so so itchy. I made myself bleed from scratching before I decided to go to the doctor. It was so easy to fix. A pill and some cream. I thought I had herpes. — Mary, 16

— "Someone told me lesbians don't get STIs. But then I got Chlamydia off this girl at camp" — Deb, 17

Going To The Doctor Without Your Parents

Going to a doctor alone, especially if it's the same doctor you've been going to for years as a kid and one who knows your whole family and stuff like that, can be daunting. But you are allowed to do it at pretty much any age. The doctor will have to determine if you are mature enough understand what they are saying to you and about what treatments they may be giving you, but there is no legal age limit. Doctors are bound by law not to tell anyone about what you say to them but there are a few exceptions. If you have a serious infectious disease, like malaria or cholera or HIV/AIDS for example, they are required to tell the Department of Health. If they believe you are in danger of harming yourself or others, or they believe you are in danger from violence or abuse they will have to contact the Department of Child Safety or similar organisations in order to protect you. A doctor can be trusted to talk to you, help you and give you all sorts of different advice on all sorts of medical and personal issues or help you to find the right person to talk to. If you are uncomfortable seeing the family doctor it is okay to seek out someone new if that makes you feel more comfortable although I do understand this can be harder in small towns and rural areas.

To see doctors in Australia you must have a Medicare card. All Australian residents and citizens have Medicare cards and you will be registered on your parent's card. You can apply for your own card at 15 years old. If you are under 15 you can apply for a duplicate card, which is just a copy of your parent's, but in most cases you will need your parent or guardian to sign the application form.

As I mentioned above, there is no law that says how old you need to be to go and see a doctor without your parents present, but the doctor will have to be sure you are able to understand what they are saying to you, and what treatments they are giving or doing. If you are under 14, or still using your parent's Medicare card, your parents will be able to see you have accessed a doctor's services and be able to see your medical records, but after you turn 14, even if they can see you have accessed the card, Medicare cannot legally give them any information about the treatments etc without your consent. If you have your own card your parents will have no access whatsoever.

Tips for Safer Sex

Please be aware that no sex is 100% safe. There are always risks. No contraceptive is 100% effective. No situation is 100% risk free. The best thing you can do is be armed with as much information as possible, and make your choices based on that. Always understand that things can go wrong no matter how safe and careful you are, but also always remember there will be someone who can help you if you ever need that help.

- Always use a condom. Always

- Always carry condoms with you. Make sure they are in date. All condoms will have a use-by date written on the box as well as stamped on each individual wrapper. If a condom reaches its expiry date, throw it out. The latex can become degraded over time and split. It's not worth the risk. Always make sure they're in date.

- It may sound odd, but if you know you will been giving oral sex, and you won't be using a condom (you should ALWAYS use a condom) make sure you haven't just brushed or flossed your teeth. Why? Because brushing and flossing can give you small cuts and abrasions in your mouth, which can lead to fluids coming into contact with open wounds which can lead to all manner of STI infections. If you're worried about bad breath use mouthwash or chew gum or something.

- Get regularly tested. If you are sexually active you should have regular STI tests and pap tests.

- Be careful with drugs and alcohol. They can lower your inhibitions and cause you to make decisions that are not normal for you.

- Look out for your friends and make sure they look out for you.

- Remember birth control pills, and the like, will NOT stop you from getting an STI.

- If something does not feel comfortable, you have every right to stop. At any time! No means no. Always.

- Never use anything but a water-based lubricant. NO Vaseline, baby oil or other oil based products. They will break the condom.

If It's Not On, It's Not On – The Importance of Condoms

If I had a dollar for every time I heard guys say, "Wearing a condom lessens sensitivity and makes sex not feel as good," I would be rich. Seriously. It's like they somehow think people should feel sorry for their poor little sheathed penis and say, "Oh, well in that case, let me risk my entire life just so you can have slightly more sensation."

In reality, yes, it can make things a little different, but the thing is, slightly less sensitivity now is nothing like the searing pain of weeing through diseased genitals, or having a life sentence of AIDS or similar handed to you because you weren't safe. Because, in reality, if someone wants to have sex with you without a condom, chances are you are not the only person. And the other people they have slept with who have agreed to do it "bareback" have most likely agreed to it with other people as well and then those people and the ones they have slept with and so on and so on. The plain truth of it is, every time you have sex with someone without using proper protection, you are in effect having sex and swapping fluids with every other person they have ever had sex with and who knows how many people that could be.

Another thing I hear is, "Do I look sick?" but, like detailed in the section above, some STIs can have absolutely no outward symptoms at all so it really is a stupid thing to say. Seriously, girls. Please don't let anyone talk you into bareback sex. It is dangerous and life risking and just not worth it. *Ever*. If someone complains that the condom pulls against the head of their penis or foreskin (which can happen and can be really uncomfortable for guys) a small drop of lube on the head of the penis before putting the condom on can really help minimise that. Don't use too much, just a little to lubricate the end. If you use too much the condom can slip off the end of the penis and put you at risk of STIs and pregnancy.

Condoms have come a long way since their first incarnations. In the very early days (like in the time of the ancient Egyptians) condoms were made of thick linen-like material, and then later, around medieval days, replaced with animal intestines. They were usually washed out and then reused too, so really, if someone is complaining about a little piece of thin latex, maybe ask them if they'd like to use a sheep's stomach instead.

Condoms can actually be a lot of fun. They come in all sorts of colours and styles and flavours. Yes, flavours. They can be incorporated into sexy time too. How? Well, you can make it all part of your foreplay. Put them on slowly and sensually with your hands or, with a little practice, you can even use your mouth to apply them, but be aware of your teeth!

When rolling one on always remember to squeeze the air out of the tip. If you don't do this the condom can fill with air and, like using too much lube inside, slip off during sex.

No Means No

When it comes to having sex, playing around, kissing, touching, anything really, it must be consensual. That means both (or all) parties involved must agree to it. If one person is hesitant, unsure or plain out says no, then everyone involved must respect that and stop.

Anything else, coercing you into it, begging til you say yes, or just going ahead and doing it anyway is sexual assault. It does not matter what you are wearing, if you are drunk or on drugs, if you said yes to begin with but change your mind, if you flirted or whatever, it is not your fault or reason that someone does something you do not want them to do.

Slut Shaming.

What is it?

Slut shaming is the term that basically means blaming girls for being attacked, raped, assaulted and generally treated badly because of how sexually active they are, what sort of clothes they wear and how they act around guys (or girls). It is really, really common. You see and hear it all the time, and you may have probably done it yourself without even realising it. Just the distaste towards girls who have a lot of sex, or wear tight clothing or flirt a lot is slut shaming. Blaming someone for attacks against them by saying things like, "Well look at how she was dressed!" or your parents telling you, "Don't leave the house in that, what do you think people will think?" It has been around for so long most people don't even realise it is being done but the truth of the matter is, no matter what you wear, how you act or how many people you kiss, flirt with or even have sex with, does not mean you deserve to be attacked.

This is an attitude that needs to change. We, as girls, need to stand up to it. We need to say NO, it is NOT anyone's fault that bad things happened to them. The fault lies solely with the person doing the bad things. It is going to take a while for this attitude to sink in, but it starts with you, with me, with every person in the world.

A case in America really brought to light those attitudes towards girls and sexual assault still have a long way to go. In this case (The Steubenville rape case) a young girl was at a party. She was very drunk and passed out and several members of the local football team raped her. And then carried her to other parties where she was again assaulted by other boys. Not only was she attacked, these boys filmed it. And laughed about it. And posted the pictures online. Then, to add insult to injury, pretty much the entire town; men, women, girls and boys, blamed her for the attack because she was drunk. Because she didn't say "no" specifically (the girl was passed out drunk, she couldn't say anything). Simply because she was there.

Everyone (including major news outlets) was upset because the boys were "promising" members of the football team and now their futures were in jeopardy because they were charged with rape.

No one seemed to spare a thought for this poor girl who was attacked, and humiliated, and raped, and shunned by her town. But the boys, the boys were treated like some sort of heroes who had been hard done by. To use a phrase I know you will get: What the fucking fuck??

This case mostly disgusted the rest of the world but highlighted real world-wide problems with the way we see rape and assault. News anchors, celebrities, average Joe's like you and me all came out saying, "Well it's a shame... But she *was* drunk and put herself in that position." Or, "What was an under-age girl doing at the party anyway?" And even, "Well she didn't specifically say no." It was completely disturbing to hear the, "It's a shame BUT ..." speak. There is no "*BUT.*" It is NEVER the victims fault. This case is the perfect way to highlight and describe "Slut Shaming." That the girl, for whatever reason, brought the attack on herself because obviously owning a vagina is bad and wrong and having it makes the girl a slut. This is just bullshit. Utter crap and a disturbing idea that makes girls responsible for the lack of control of males. This is not a female problem. It is a male one; and on a wider scale, a societal one. It is a problem caused by old-fashioned attitudes that boys can have as much sex as they want but girls must be prim and proper and never have sex unless they are married and want to have a baby. It is absolute fucking bullshit, and, if you haven't guessed, one that makes me so angry I could spit. It is NOT your fault if a male cannot control himself. That blame should be solely on the person doing the attack and no one else.

As the final edits to this book were happening, the awful case of the Stanford rape came into the public view. This is yet another highlight of why we must speak up and speak out against rape culture. A young woman's life was ruined, and the man who is solely responsible for that was sentenced to six months, of which he will have only served three, where it was recommended he have at least six years for the horrific nature of his crime. The reasoning for his ridiculously light sentence? He is a good swimmer, and a judge didn't want to ruin his future. His future? Not a word about the young woman's future. Nothing about the pain and damage he caused to not only her body physically, but to her mind and psyche. If you haven't, search out her victim statement and read it. You can search for it on Google, and I highly recommend you do so. It will break your heart, it will make you squirm uncomfortably, and it will make you cry. And it will show you how far we still have to go. Use the fire it creates in you to stand up for your friends. To look out for them. To stand up against this illogical idea that because a boy is good at sport he can basically get away with anything. I mean come on, it's so utterly unbelievable, and yet it happens all the time.

You can be walking down the street fully naked and no one has the right to touch you. You could have had sex a hundred times before, in public, on a big glittery stage for the world to see, and no one has the right to touch you without your consent. Women have been raped while wearing jeans, or a burqa, or overalls or miniskirts or in fancy dress and it is never their fault. If a person robs a bank and shoots a bank teller is it the teller's fault for working in a bank? Have you ever heard anyone tell the victim of a carjacking that it was their fault for owning a car? No. You wouldn't because the concept is laughable. It is solely the fault of the person holding up the bank or robbing the car driver. It is the same with sexual assault. The blame is only ever on the attacker. And should never be on the victim.

Because of these attitudes, rape and other sexual assaults are often not reported because girls are so ashamed and afraid of the backlash they will get and the questions they may have to answer puts them off going to the police and making a report. Questions like, "What were you wearing?" "Were you drunk?" "How many sexual partners have you had?" Again, this is bullshit. And it must end with us. With people who have had enough of the blame and enough of the fear. So think about it. Next time you see a pissed girl at a party with boys all over her, what will you do? Will you turn away in disgust and call her a slut and write horrible things about her on Facebook? Or will you go to her aid? Let people know it isn't right. Maybe save a life? The same goes for a girl who is having lots of sex with full consent. So what if she enjoys it? It isn't your place to judge her, just as you would hate to be judged for anything you do.

It's a hard lesson to unlearn, I know. But it is a good one. One that will make you a better person. A better adult. A decent human being.

Where to get help.

Unfortunately, no matter what we do, what we wear, how we "protect" ourselves, sexual assault happens. If it has happened to you, or someone you know, or even if you've seen or heard something that just didn't feel right, it's important to speak out. In these situations there are quite a few avenues you can take. Firstly, you must tell someone. An adult you trust. A teacher or older sibling or your parents. There are help lines and websites you can go to (all listed in the back section of this book) and there are also the police. I know speaking out can be hard, and going to the police can be a scary and intimidating thing, but there are youth officers and police officers trained and specialised in sexual assault cases and they are there to help you.

It is also really important to know that not all abuse is sexual or physical. Abuse comes in many forms and all of it can have a huge impact on your self-esteem and your whole life. Physical violence, verbal abuse, mental abuse, these are all real things and in a relationship they can often start quite slowly so you don't even notice it's happening until it's too late. There are a few little things you can look out for, although I know when you are in a new relationship, it's very easy to get caught up in the awesomeness that is new love to be able to see clearly what's happening. Here is a simple checklist to keep in mind that may help you recognise the signs that things might go somewhere less than positive.

Over Possessiveness: In a new relationship it is completely understandable that you want to spend every minute of the day with that person, however you really do

Signs to look out for in abusive and controlling relationships;

- Puts you down. Whether it's about how you look. How you act. How you dress. How you speak.

- Deliberately embarrasses you or humiliates you to other people

- Is unreasonably jealous.

- Isolates you from friends and family, often using the excuse that they are "unhealthy" or "bad for you", or that it "takes you away from them"

- Makes threats. These don't even have to be physical threats. They can be as simple as "If you do/don't do (x) then I will do (x).

need time for yourself, with your friends, and with your family. If a partner starts to make you feel bad about these things, or tries to keep you from seeing friends and family, this can be a sign that their possessiveness could get dangerous.

Put downs and mean comments about you, whether they are about your looks, your weight, your personality, your intelligence, anything, these are not okay. Sometimes these things can be really subtle but if someone makes you feel bad, if they make it out that no one but them will love you/go out with you etc, then these are all signs of abuse.

Physical violence is never okay and if it ever happens you must seek help immediately. It doesn't matter if they say they are sorry. If they say you deserved it or if they promise never to do it again. Violence, emotional blackmail, mean comments are all huge signs that something is wrong and you must absolutely talk to someone and seek help.

These are all very telling signs and can be very subtle and hard to pinpoint. This is how the cycle of abuse stays and grows into really dangerous situations. If you feel at all like you may identify with any of these points it is super important to talk to someone. Your mum, an older sister or friend, even a teacher or counsellor. It is vitally important to remember that your feelings are very real and quite often if we feel like something is wrong, it often is.

So What about This Whole Feminism Thing?

"Feminism Is The Radical Notion That Women Are People."

Marie Shear (writer, editor, feminist)

So many times I hear young women, famous women, school girls; women from all walks of life say things like, "I'm not a feminist." Or, "I don't need feminism." But we do. We ALL do. Everyone single one of us including men.

Feminism is not a dirty word. It is not a word that means you hate men. It does not mean you hate sex. It doesn't mean you cannot be a stay at home mother or enjoy wearing make up. Feminism doesn't mean you cannot shave your armpits or squeal over a cool pair of shoes. Feminism doesn't mean anything at all about any of those things. Feminism is about women being equal to men. Not better than, not superior to, not full of hatred towards, no. Just plain equality in a world that leans so heavily towards the privilege of men.

If you believe you have the right to walk down a street without being touched by a stranger, then you are a feminist. If you believe little girls should not be told they have to grow up and find a husband to be worth anything in this world, then you are a feminist. If you believe a little girl can be both a princess and Darth Vader then you are a feminist. If you believe that girls and women are more than the sum of what they look like and how their body looks, then you are a feminist.

If you believe in the rights of women and girls to have education and healthcare, the right to choose what happens to their own bodies. If you believe that the genitals you have should have no bearing on the life you lead, the job you do, the person you love, the world you live in, then you are a feminist.

So, the next time you hear (or even think or say yourself), "I am not a feminist because ..." Remember this one thing: The very fact you can stand up and say that, without being put in jail or have rocks thrown at you, the very fact you have the skills and ability to pick up this book and read the words I am typing, the very fact you can choose to be a physicist or a park ranger or a pole dancer, or all three at the same time, the very fact you can buy a house, have your own money, drive a car, speak your mind ... THAT is why you *are* a feminist and why feminism still exists.

Phone numbers, Websites, and Services

A lot of these are websites, which I know you can't "click on" in a book, but because so much is online these days, and we basically have the internet in our pockets all the time, it is really important that I put the websites here. Googling the names of the organisations will bring up the pages instead of having to enter the long web addresses. But you can do that too.

Please use these services when you need to talk or learn or be informed. They are there to help you!

Police Emergency – Phone 000

Mental Health Support

Lifeline (24/7): 13 11 14 - They can help put you in contact with crisis centres and other help facilities in your state

Kids Helpline: Free call 1800 551 800. They also have online website counselling at www.kidshelp.com.au

Headspace (Open 9am-5pm): headspace.org.au

Reach Out: reachout.com

Beyond Blue: beyondblue.org.au

Wesley LifeForce Service Finder.

Although it is run by the Uniting Church, this resource is not religiously tilted. You can enter a state, area or postcode to find a wealth of services from mental health, youth services, rape crisis. LGBTIQA services and other emergency numbers.

www.wesleymission.org.au/wesleylifeforceservicefinder

Sexual Health and Family Planning (SHFP) Clinics

A.C.T

SHFPACT

Level One, 28 University Ave, Canberra

Email: shfpact@shfpact.org.au

Phone : 02 6247 3077

Website: http://www.shfpact.org.au

NSW

Family Planning NSW

http://www.fpnsw.org.au

Ashfeild - 328 - 336 Liverpool Road, (02) 8752 4316

Dubbo - 2B / 155 Macquarie St, (02) 6885 1544

Fairfield - 24 - 26 Nelson Street, (02) 9754 1322

Newcastle - 384 Hunter Street, (02) 4929 4485

Penrith - 13 Reserve Street, (02) 4749 0500

N.T

Family Planning Welfare Association of the Northern Territory

Darwin, Coconut Grove - Unit 2, The Clock Tower, Dick Ward Drive, (08) 8948 0144

Palmerston, Specialist Suites, Cnr. Temple Tce & Roystonea Ave

Contact Darwin Head office for appointments

QLD

Family Planning Queensland

Fortitude Valley - 100 Alfred Street

Cairns - Ground Floor Solander Centre, 182 Grafton St

Ipswich - Shop 5/54 Limestone Street

Rockhampton - 83 Bolsover Street

Toowomba - First Floor, 4 Duggan Street

SA

SHine SA

Woodville - Woodville GP Plus Health Care Centre, 64c Woodville Road

Hillcrest - Gilles Plains GP Plus Super Clinic, 1 Gilles Crescent

Salisbury - Shopfront Youth Health & Information Service, Shop 4, 72 John Street

Oaklands Park, GP Plus Health Care Centre Marion, 10 Milham Street (across from Aquatic Centre)

Noarlunga - GP Plus Super Clinic Noarlunga (Level 1),

20 Alexander Kelly Drive

Davoren Park - 43 Peachey Road,

TAS

Family Planning Tasmania

Glenorchy - 421 Main Road, Glenorchy TAS 7010

Launceston - 269 Wellington Street, Launceston, 7250

Upper Bernie - 1 Pine Ave, Upper Burnie

VIC

Family Planning, Victoria

Box Hill, Ground floor, 901 Whitehorse Rd, Box Hill (near Box Hill Station), Phone: 03 9257 0100 or freecall: 1800 013 952

Melbourne CBD - Action Centre Level 1, 94 Elizabeth St, Melbourne (near Flinders St Station)

Hoppers Crossing - Youth Resource Centre 86 Derrimut Rd, Hoppers Crossing

WA

Family Planning WA

Northbridge;

70 Roe Street, Northbridge WA 6003

170 Aberdeen Street, Northbridge WA 6003

Free Sexual Health Clinics

A really fast way to search for a clinic in your local area is to go to these websites and put in your location and they will bring up every resource available in your area. This is particularly useful for people in isolated or rural areas who may not know what services are available in their local area.

www.couldihaveit.com.au This is a brilliant resource with clinics, information, support services and phone numbers and websites.

www.bettertoknow.org.au A wonderful resource of clinics, websites, information and tips.

www.reachout.com Search "sexual health clinics"in the search bar and a Q&A article has links to clinics and services by state.

Or go to these websites for all the locations and information in your states

Victoria

Melbourne Sexual Health Centre - www.mshc.org.au

New South Wales

www.health.nsw.gov.au/sexualhealth/Pages/sexual-health-clinics.aspx, (this page has a map with every location of clinics set out for you)

Queensland

www.health.qld.gov.au/clinical-practice/guidelines-procedures/sex-health/services, (Government page with links to all sexual health clinics as well as other sexual health services)

Tasmania

www.dhhs.tas.gov.au/sexualhealth/sexual_health_service_tasmania, (Government page with links to all sexual health clinics as well as other sexual health services)

Northern Territory

https://nt.gov.au/wellbeing/hospitals-health-services/sexual-health-services/clinic-34

(Government page with links to Clinic 34, a Northern Territory free sexual health service)

South Australia

www.sahealth.sa.gov.au/wps/wcm/connect/Public+Content/SA+Health+Internet/Health+services/Sexual+health+services/

(Government page with links to all sexual health clinics as well as other sexual health services)

Western Australia

www.health.wa.gov.au/services/category.cfm?Topic_ID=8, (Government page with links to all sexual health clinics as well as other sexual health services)

ACT

www.health.act.gov.au/our-services/sexual-health/act-sexual-health-contacts, (Government page with links to all sexual health clinics as well as other sexual health services)

LGBTIQA Support

www.minus18.org.au – Australia wide support, mentoring and mental health services. Social groups. Resources. Networking

www.pflagaustralia.org.au – Parents and Friends of Lesbian and Gay Australians. A non profit voluntary organisation with the the common goal of keeping families together

www.lgbthealth.org.au – An Australia wide coalition of health services and health-related organisations targeted at LGBTIQA Australians.

www.samesame.com.au – Support. News. Forums.

www.comingout.com.au – Help and support and information on coming out.

FTMShed http://www.transshedboys.com/ -We are a Melbourne based support group for trans masculine people and their allies.

Seahorse Victoria - http://seahorsevic.com.au/main/

Seahorse Victoria Inc was formed in 1975 as a support and social group for the Victorian transgender community

Zoe Belle Gender Centre http://www.zbgc.com.au/ Promoting well-being for the trans and gender diverse community of Victoria since 2007

Eva's End Note

Sex really is a crazy, complicated, fun, exciting and interesting thing. Even armed with all the information in the world you're going to come across barriers and hurdles and things you haven't planned for. But really, that's life. That's what it's about. Taking each day and each new adventure by the hand and saying, "Let's do this funky thang!" Everything we do, every time we do it, is a new and exciting experience and the best advice I can give you is to be safe. Be wise. And be prepared. Be aware that things don't always go to plan and that sometimes things turn out differently than you had expected. Sometimes that's a bad thing, and sometimes a good thing. But always know there is a bunch of help, advice, love and support to be found. Seek out information wherever you go in life. Always be willing to listen, learn and find new ways of looking at things. Be happy with who you are and live your life to the fullest. Remember you are beautiful. You are normal. And most of all, you are you and that's a pretty damn good thing to be.

ABOUT THE AUTHOR

Eva Sless in an award-winning Australian writer with a passion for sex education and sex positivity.

Starting her writing career with a personal column about life as a sex worker in the Australian adult magazine "People", she was quickly recognised as a voice that was inclusive and educating without being patronising. Her talents have been picked up by The Australian Sex Party, Australian Penthouse, Adult Matchmaker, and the online young feminist magazine Birdee.

From sex toy reviews to discussions of feminism and BDSM, Eva focuses on the pleasure and consent sided of sex education, as well as being a strong advocate for LGBTI youth, the Safe Schools Program and anything that allows kids to be free to express themselves and their identities, be it sexual or gender based.

She lives a very healthy, happy and settled non-monogamous life in the sunshine by the water with her husband, daughter and psycho cat. She enjoys long binge sessions with Netflix, eating Tim Tams and getting into feminist and political arguments with idiots on Facebook and Twitter!

CPSIA information can be obtained
at www.ICGtesting.com
Printed in the USA
BVHW041208130519
548121BV00016B/1152/P

9 780992 351427